Ramen Noodle Soup And Vietnamese Cookbook

2 Books In 1: Over 150 Recipes Cookbook For Classic Asian Comfort Food

By

Maki Blanc

RAMEN
COOKBOOK

70 Recipes for Preparing at Home Traditional Japanese Noodle Soup.

By

Maki Blanc

© **Copyright 2021 by Maki Blanc - All rights reserved.**

This document is geared towards providing exact and reliable information in regard to the topic and issue covered. The publication is sold with the idea that the publisher is not required to render accounting, officially permitted, or otherwise, qualified services. If advice is necessary, legal or professional, a practiced individual in the profession should be ordered.

From a Declaration of Principles which was accepted and approved equally by a Committee of the American Bar Association and a Committee of Publishers and Associations.

In no way is it legal to reproduce, duplicate, or transmit any part of this document in either electronic means or in printed format. Recording of this publication is strictly prohibited and any storage of this document is not allowed unless with written permission from the publisher. All rights reserved.

The information provided herein is stated to be truthful and consistent, in that any liability, in terms of inattention or otherwise, by any usage or abuse of any policies, processes, or directions contained within is the solitary and utter responsibility of the recipient reader. Under no circumstances will any legal responsibility or blame be held against the publisher for any reparation, damages, or monetary loss due to the information herein, either directly or indirectly.

Respective authors own all copyrights not held by the publisher.

The information herein is offered for informational purposes solely and is universal as so. The presentation of the information is without contract or any type of guarantee assurance.

The trademarks that are used are without any consent, and the publication of the trademark is without permission or backing by the trademark owner. All trademarks and brands within this book are for clarifying purposes only and are owned by the owners themselves, not affiliated with this document.

Contents

INTRODUCTION 12

CHAPTER 1: INTRODUCTION TO JAPANESE NOODLE SOUPS 14

1.1 History and Origin of Ramen 14

1.2 Ramen According to the Nutrition and Dietetics 16

1.3 Various Ingredients Used in Ramen 17

CHAPTER 2: THE WORLD OF RAMEN BREAKFAST RECIPES 20

2.1 Japanese Ramen Scrambled Eggs Recipe 21

2.2 Japanese Bacon and Egg Ramen Recipe 22

2.3 Japanese Ramen Omelet Recipe 24

2.4 Japanese Ramen with Soft Boiled Eggs Recipe 25

2.5 Japanese Miso Ramen with Boiled Eggs Recipe 27

2.6 Japanese Bacon, Egg and Cheese Breakfast Ramen Recipe 28

2.7 Japanese Ramen with Tofu and Eggs Recipe 30

2.8 Japanese Chicken Ramen with Bok Choy and Soy Eggs Recipe 32

2.9 Japanese Egg Tonkotsu Ramen Recipe 33

2.10 Japanese Scallops and Egg Ramen Recipe 34

CHAPTER 3: THE WORLD OF RAMEN LUNCH RECIPES 37

3.1 Japanese Ramen Noodle Soup Recipe 37

3.2 Japanese Duck Ramen Recipes 39

3.3 Japanese Sapporo Ramen Recipe 40

3.4 Japanese Miso Ramen Recipe 42

3.5 Japanese Shoyu Ramen Recipe 43

3.6 Japanese Tantanmen Ramen Recipe 45

3.7 Japanese Spicy Pork Ramen Recipe 46

3.8 Japanese Roast Pork Ramen Recipe 48

3.9 Japanese Chargrilled Chicken Ramen Recipe 49

3.10 Japanese Lemongrass, Chicken and Ginger Ramen Recipe 51

3.11 Japanese Spicy Beef Ramen Recipe 52

3.12 Japanese Prawn Ramen Recipe 54

3.13 Japanese Ramen Noodle Salad Recipe 56

3.14 Japanese Mongolian Beef Ramen Recipe 57

3.15 Japanese Meatball Ramen Recipe 59

3.16 Japanese Ramen Noodle Skillet with Steak Recipe 60

3.17 Japanese Cheese Ramen Recipe 62

3.18 Japanese Ramen Burger Recipe 64

3.19 Japanese Garlic and Shrimp Ramen Recipe 66

3.20 Japanese Beef and Ramen Stir-Fry Recipe 67

CHAPTER 4: THE WORLD OF RAMEN DINNER RECIPES 70

4.1 Japanese Parmesan and Garlic Ramen Recipe 70

4.2 Japanese Ginger and Beef Stir-Fry Ramen Recipe 72

4.3 Japanese Peanut and Chicken Ramen Recipe 73

4.4 Japanese Roasted Chicken Ramen Recipe 75

4.5 Japanese Sirarcha and Shrimp Ramen Recipe 77

4.6 Japanese Bacon Ramen Soup Recipe 79

4.7 Japanese Sweet and Sour Pork Ramen Recipe 81

4.8 Japanese Cheesy Tuna Ramen Recipe 82

4.9 Japanese Ramen and Tomato Soup Recipe 85

4.10 Japanese Chili Ramen Recipe 86

4.11 Japanese Chicken and Mushroom Ramen Recipe 88

4.12 Japanese Parmesan Chicken Ramen Recipe 89

4.13 Japanese Chicken Lo Mein Ramen Recipe 91

4.14 Japanese Shrimp Ramen Recipe 92

4.15 Japanese Green Pepper and Chicken Ramen Recipe 94

4.16 Japanese Creamy Tonkotsu Ramen Recipe 97

4.17 Japanese Miso and Crispy Pork Ramen Recipe 98

4.18 Japanese Shio and Pork Ramen Recipe 100

4.19 Japanese Ramen Noodle Coleslaw Recipe 102

4.20 Japanese Instant Ramen Noodle Recipe 103

CHAPTER 5: THE WORLD OF VEGETARIAN RAMEN RECIPES 104

5.1 Japanese Spicy Vegetarian Ramen Recipe 104

5.2 Japanese Shiitake Mushroom Ramen Recipe 105

5.3 Japanese Miso Vegetarian Ramen Noodle Soup Recipe 107

5.4 Japanese Teriyaki Tofu Ramen Recipe 109

5.5 Japanese Tonkotsu Vegetarian Ramen Recipe 110

5.6 Japanese Pantry Vegetarian Ramen Recipe 112

5.7 Japanese Marinated Tofu and Vegetable Ramen Recipe 113

5.8 Japanese Creamy Vegan Ramen Recipe 115

5.9 Japanese Creamy Sesame Ramen Broth Recipe 116

5.10 Japanese Spicy Broccoli Ramen Recipe 118

5.11 Japanese Cauliflower Ramen Recipe 119

5.12 Japanese Hot and Sour Dashi Ramen Recipe 121

5.13 Japanese Spicy Carrot Ramen Recipe 122

5.14 Japanese Vegan Shōyu Ramen with Potatoes Recipe 123

5.15 Japanese Ginger Ramen Recipe 126

5.16 Japanese Vegan Ramen Taco Recipe 127

5.17 Japanese Vegetarian Spicy Peanut Tempeh Ramen Recipe
.... 128

5.18 Japanese Spicy Soy Milk Ramen Recipe 129

5.19 Japanese Vegetarian Ginger and Scallion Ramen Recipe 131

5.20 Japanese Crispy Sesame Tofu Ramen Recipe 132

CONCLUSION 134

INTRODUCTION 138

CHAPTER 1: THE WORLD OF VIETNAMESE BREAKFAST RECIPES 139

1.1 Vietnamese Fried Egg Recipe 139

1.2 Vietnamese Breakfast Burgers Recipe 140

1.3 Vietnamese Steamed Rice Rolls with Pork Recipe 141

1.4 Vietnamese Crepes Recipe 142

1.5 Vietnamese Breakfast Bowl Recipe 143

1.6 Vietnamese Happy Pancakes Recipe 144

1.7 Vietnamese Breakfast Pastries Recipe 145

1.8 Vietnamese Scrambled Eggs with Fish Sauce Recipe 146

1.9 Vietnamese Steak and Eggs Recipe 147

1.10 Vietnamese Scrambled Eggs with Pork Mince Recipe 148

1.11 Vietnamese Breakfast Egg Rolls Recipe 149

1.12 Vietnamese Tofu Pancakes Recipe 150

CHAPTER 2: THE WORLD OF VIETNAMESE LUNCH RECIPES 152

2.1 Vietnamese Prawn and Papaya Salad Recipe 152

2.2 Vietnamese Chicken Salad Recipes 153

2.3 Vietnamese Herb Salad Recipe 154

2.4 Vietnamese Summer Rolls with Peanut Dipping Sauce Recipe
.... 155

2.5 Vietnamese Pork Meatballs Recipe 156

2.6 Vietnamese Chicken Pho Recipe **157**

2.7 Vietnamese Baked Snapper Recipe...**158**

2.8 Vietnamese Stir-Fried Sweet Shrimp Recipe **160**

2.9 Vietnamese Lemongrass and Tamarind Chicken Recipe **161**

2.10 Vietnamese Marinated Lamb Chops Recipe **162**

2.11 Vietnamese Cabbage Soup Recipe..**163**

2.12 Vietnamese Mixed Vegetables Recipe..**164**

2.13 Vietnamese Fried Rice Recipe..**165**

2.14 Vietnamese Pork Chops Recipe **167**

2.15 Vietnamese Instant Pho Soup Recipe **168**

CHAPTER 3: THE WORLD OF VIETNAMESE DINNER RECIPES **170**

3.1 Vietnamese Sambal Kangkung with Shrimp Paste Recipe **170**

3.2 Vietnamese Pomelo and Shrimp Salad Recipe **171**

3.3 Vietnamese Pork Bone and Green Papaya Soup Recipe **172**

3.4 Vietnamese Beef and Noodle Salad Recipe.................................**173**

3.5 Vietnamese Lamb Shanks with Sweet Potatoes Recipe.............**174**

3.6 Vietnamese Spiced Duck Salad Recipe **176**

3.7 Vietnamese Seafood Salad Recipe...**177**

3.8 Vietnamese Caramel Trout Recipe..**177**

3.9 Vietnamese Veggie Hotpot Recipe **179**

3.10 Vietnamese Prawn and Noodle Salad with Crispy Shallots Recipe **180**

3.11 Vietnamese Lemongrass Chicken Recipe 181

3.12 Vietnamese Garlic Butter Noodles Recipe 182

3.13 Vietnamese Papaya Salad Recipe 183

3.14 Vietnamese Purple Yam Soup Recipe 184

3.15 Vietnamese Fried Tofu Recipe 185

3.16 Vietnamese Noodle Soup Recipe 186

3.17 Vietnamese Shaking Beef Recipe 187

3.18 Vietnamese Tomato and Pineapple Fish Soup Recipe 188

CHAPTER 4: THE WORLD OF VIETNAMESE DESSERT RECIPES 190

4.1 Vietnamese Pandan Rice and Mung Bean Cake Recipe 190

4.2 Vietnamese Peanut Sticky Rice Recipe 191

4.3 Vietnamese Mung Bean Dumplings Recipe 192

4.4 Vietnamese Pandan Waffles Recipe 193

4.5 Vietnamese Three Color Dessert Recipe 194

4.6 Vietnamese Fruit Cocktail Recipe 196

4.7 Vietnamese Sweet Corn Pudding Recipe 196

4.8 Vietnamese Banana Tapioca Recipe 197

4.9 Vietnamese Sesame Balls Recipe 199

4.10 Vietnamese Sponge Cake Recipe 200

4.11 Vietnamese Milkshake Recipe 200

4.12 Vietnamese Ice Cream Recipe 201

4.13 Vietnamese Taro Pudding Recipe 202

4.14 Vietnamese Sticky Rice Recipe 203

4.15 Vietnamese Donuts Recipe 204

CHAPTER 5: THE WORLD OF VIETNAMESE SNACK RECIPES 206

5.1 Crispy Vietnamese Fish Cakes Recipe 206

5.2 Crispy Vietnamese Lettuce Cups Recipe 207

5.3 Vietnamese Beef and Mango Salad Recipe 208

5.4 Vietnamese Prawn and Lime Mayo Wrap Recipe 209

5.5 Vietnamese Rice Paper Rolls Recipe 211

5.6 Vietnamese Pickled Bitter Melon Salad Recipe 212

5.7 Vietnamese Spring Rolls Recipe 213

5.8 Vietnamese Chicken Baguettes Recipe 214

5.9 Vietnamese Fish Sauce Recipe 215

5.10 Vietnamese Shrimp Tacos Recipe 216

CONCLUSION 219

Introduction

Ramen are the most famous noodle dishes in Japan. These boiled noodles are essentially served in various flavorful soups with numerous toppings. Chukamen noodles which are for the most part made with wheat flour and kansui are used for ramen dishes. There are numerous types of ramen flavors in Japan. They are used in different flavors of soups, garnishes, broth, noodle texture in ramens, and this is only the tip of an iceberg. Making a tasty ramen is not very simple if you are preparing it from scratch.

The flavor of ramen predominantly relies upon the soup. Ramen cooks generally train themselves for quite a while to be able to make great ramen soup. Each ramen shop has its own particular manner to make ramen soup. So, there are countless ways to make ramen soup. Chicken bone, pork bone, dried sardines, as well as kombu are utilized to make soup stock for ramen.

You can prepare Japanese ramen soup at home by learning the list of various ingredients that you will need to start cooking. By reading this wonderful book, you will get the detailed knowledge regarding the nutritional value and history of ramen. This book contains over 70 different breakfast, lunch, dinner, and vegetarian ramen recipes. You can easily start cooking at home with the detailed instructions present below each recipe. So start reading and start cooking today!

Chapter 1: Introduction to Japanese Noodle Soups

Ramen is a noodle soup dish that was initially imported from China and has become perhaps the most mainstream dishes in Japan for the past many years. Ramen are cheap and broadly accessible. These two factors additionally make them an ideal choice for tourists. Ramen cafés can be found in each corner of the country. These cafes produce incalculable varieties of this basic noodle dish.

Typical Ramen noodles are long and flexible. However, innumerable assortments of ramen exist that vary from slender to thick and wavy. Some ramen cafes permit you to modify your noodle soup in many ways, for example, by permitting you to choose its thickness (slight, ordinary or thick) or doneness (normal or firm).

1.1 History and Origin of Ramen

The ramen noodle has extended its compass across numerous lands and nations framing profound roots in many of these societies. Actually, the noodle has effectively managed to form connections with Japan's lifestyle and history as well. Ramen has a long history in Japan, changing as the conditions of the nation changed too.

The origin of the first ramen is obscure. Yet, a legend says that ramen came from a dish acquired from China. The principal legend sets up Shu Shunsui, a researcher from China, as the person who brought the ramen formula to Japan.

Shu Shunsui was a Chinese exile of the Ming government who came to fill in as a consultant to the Japanese primitive master Tokugawa Mitsukuni. Verifiable records show that Shu Shunsui advised Mitsukini on what to add to his udon soup to make it taste better. This dish is supposed to be the first ramen that was eaten in Japan. While the facts confirm that Chinese culture vigorously affected Japanese culture at that time. Yet, an authentic record of Mitsukini cooking ramen does not exist.

Another legend interfaces the origin of ramen. It happened when Japan opened its ports to the rest of the world. Japan's ports pulled in Chinese voyagers, and a Chinese noodle soup called laa-mein was brought into Japan. This dish fills in as a possible archetype to the ramen today even though laa-mein did not have any garnishes and was not like the advanced ramen.

The last and most conceivable hypothesis relates the source of the ramen to a shop called Rai Ken in Tokyo during the 1900s. Rai Ken utilized Chinese laborers and served a noodle dish called Shina Soba. Shina Soba had added fixings that looked like todays ramen. These fixings include cooked pork, Japanese fish cake, and nori sheets into one dish. Japan was getting industrialized and more urbanized during this timeframe. Japan's industrialization and urbanization helped in promoting ramen. Shina soba was a modest and filling dish, giving a lot of calories to Japanese metropolitan laborers.

Today ramen has become an image and chronicled figure of Japanese culture and history. Ramen has broadened its span universally all throughout the planet.

Conventional ramen is extremely necessary in Japanese culture. In any case, it is still difficult to get credible Japanese ramen except if one is close to the huge assorted urban communities. Now, ramen can be found at practically any general store. Despite the fact that ramen has now become a worldwide pattern, its profound roots will consistently be appended to Japan's set of experiences.

1.2 Ramen According to the Nutrition and Dietetics

The conventional Japanese eating routine is full of healthy food sources. It has all the basic macronutrients that are essential for a healthy and nutritious diet. Japanese traditional cuisine depends on conventional Japanese cooking, otherwise called "washoku." This cooking comprises of adding fresh and healthy ingredients into the dishes to make sure the health of the individuals is not compromised. This eating design is rich in supplements and may give various medical advantages. These advantages may include improved weight reduction, digestion and absorption, long life span, and overall health.

Ramen noodles are the healthiest when joined with different fixings to make a nutritious feast. Ramen is incredible to use as a base for a variety of healthy dishes and it is not difficult to prepare on your own. Ramen noodles are healthy as they contain protein and carbohydrates in good amounts. Fats are present in a very low quantity that is almost negligible.

You can also add vegetables in your bowl of ramen. This will add to a generous flavor and add supplements to the supper. Carrots, spinach, broccoli, zucchini, cauliflower and peppers will not just give you extraordinary taste, they will give you a decent serving of vitamins, minerals and fiber in each bite. Try adding various blends of vegetables with various ramen flavors to discover the combination that you like the best. Ramen bowls consistently go extraordinary with fresh chicken, beef meat, fish or pork for the protein your body needs.

Investigate the possibilities and look at how easy it is to change a generally extraordinary tasting and healthy bowl of ramen noodles into an even healthier feast in minutes by adding different ingredients into it.

1.3 Various Ingredients Used in Ramen

Following are the different ingredients that are used in making ramen noodles at home:

1. Stocks

Stocks are generally from pork or chicken bones or a combination of the two. Dashi stock is made utilizing bonito chips which is a dried fish. Rather than making your own stock, you can purchase instant dashi stock sachets.

2. Mirin

Mirin is a Japanese sweet rice wine, which is currently broadly accessible in the global food walkways of most of the stores. It has a sweet surface and adds pleasant flavor to a dish.

3. Sake

Japanese sake is utilized in numerous Japanese dishes. However, you can use a substitute Chinese Shaoxing rice wine, which is more broadly accessible. Shaoxing rice wine adds another layer when utilizing delicate flavors in Japanese and Chinese cooking and is fabulous for adding flavor to meat when cooking and in marinades.

4. Nori sheets

Nori sheets are very healthy and usually used in different ramen dishes. They add protein into the ramen. They have an incredible flavor and are loved by many people around the world.

5. Kimchi

This is a Korean derived dish. It is fermented cabbage that is used in ramen noodles as a side dish. Kimchi adds a salty and tangy flavor into the ramen noodles.

6. Japanese curry sauce

These curry sauce packets contain a bar of curry concentrate, which can be broken off in pieces and added to stock bases for a curried broth. The flavor is similar to a Chinese curry paste and makes a great delicately flavored curry broth. It is commonly used in ramen noodles.

7. Soy sauce

It is the most common sauce all around the world. It is added to ramen noodles and imparts a unique taste to the noodles. Soy sauce comes in two varieties i.e. light soy sauce and dark soy sauce.

Chapter 2: The World of Ramen Breakfast Recipes

Having Ramen for breakfast is customary in two districts of Japan, and many nearby ramen shops carry on this tradition. These districts are Fukushima and Kitakata. All the breakfast dishes mentioned below are healthy and are traditionally eaten in these districts of Japan:

Basic Instructions to Cook Ramen:

- Take a large saucepan.
- Add water into the saucepan.
- Boil the water.
- Add the ramen noodles when the water reaches the boiling temperature.
- Cook the ramen for seven minutes approximately.
- Make sure not to overcook the ramen noodles.
- Drain the noodles and add a teaspoon of oil into the ramen.
- The oil will prevent the ramen from sticking.
- You can use this method of boiling the ramen in all of the recipes below.

2.1 Japanese Ramen Scrambled Eggs Recipe

Preparation Time: 30 minutes
Cooking Time: 10 minutes
Serving: 4

Ingredients:

- Chopped chives, one teaspoon
- Butter, two tablespoon
- Cooked chickpeas, half cup
- Tofu cubes, half pound
- Salt, to taste
- Black pepper, to taste
- Tamari paste, two teaspoon
- Eggs, four
- Mirin paste, one tablespoon
- Chopped garlic, one teaspoon
- Ramen noodles, four packs

Instructions:
1. Take a large pan.
2. Add the butter and let it meltdown.
3. Add in the eggs.
4. Add in the tamari paste.

5. Mix the tamari paste and eggs.
6. Add the chopped garlic.
7. Scramble the mixture.
8. Add in the salt and pepper.
9. Add in the chickpeas and rest of the ingredients in the end.
10. Boil the ramen noodles according to the instructions on the pack.
11. Drain the noodles and add them into the pan.
12. Mix all the ingredients well and then dish them out.
13. Garnish the fresh chopped chives on top.
14. Your dish is ready to be served.

2.2 Japanese Bacon and Egg Ramen Recipe

Preparation Time: 30 minutes
Cooking Time: 10 minutes
Serving: 4

Ingredients:

- Chopped chives, one teaspoon
- Butter, two tablespoon
- Chopped bacon, half pound
- Salt, to taste

- Black pepper, to taste
- Tamari paste, two teaspoon
- Eggs, four
- Mirin paste, one tablespoon
- Chopped garlic, one teaspoon
- Ramen noodles, four packs

Instructions:
1. Take a large pan.
2. Add the butter and let it meltdown.
3. Add in the chopped bacons.
4. Add in the tamari paste.
5. Mix all the ingredients well.
6. Add the chopped garlic.
7. Add in the rest of the ingredients in the end.
8. Scramble the mixture.
9. Add in the salt and pepper.
10. Boil the ramen noodles according to the instructions on the pack.
11. Drain the noodles and add them into the pan.
12. Mix all the ingredients well and then dish them out.
13. Garnish the fresh chopped chives on top.
14. Your dish is ready to be served.

2.3 Japanese Ramen Omelet Recipe

Preparation Time: 30 minutes
Cooking Time: 10 minutes
Serving: 4

Ingredients:

- Onions, half cup
- Rice wine, one tablespoon
- Eggs, four
- Black pepper, to taste
- Salt, to taste
- Starch, a quarter teaspoon
- Ramen noodles, four packs
- Ginger, one slice
- Soy sauce, one tablespoon
- Oil, one tablespoon
- Cilantro, as required

Instructions:
1. Take a large bowl.
2. Add all the ingredients into the bowl.

3. Make the egg mixture.
4. Take a large pan.
5. Heat a pan and then add the oil into the pan.
6. Add the egg mixture on top when the oil heats up.
7. Let the eggs cook from the bottom.
8. Now slowly start to flip the egg.
9. Dish out the egg when both the sides turn golden brown.
10. Garnish the eggs by adding chopped cilantro on top.
11. Your dish is ready to be served.

2.4 Japanese Ramen with Soft Boiled Eggs Recipe

Preparation Time: 30 minutes

Cooking Time: 10 minutes

Serving: 4

Ingredients:

- Chopped chives, one teaspoon
- Butter, two tablespoon
- Salt, to taste
- Black pepper, to taste
- Tamari paste, two teaspoon
- Eggs, four

- Mirin paste, one tablespoon
- Chopped garlic, one teaspoon
- Ramen noodles, four packs

Instructions:
1. Boil the eggs.
2. Make sure to boil the eggs for five minutes only.
3. Take a large pan.
4. Add the butter and let it meltdown.
5. Add in the tamari paste.
6. Mix all the ingredients well.
7. Add the chopped garlic.
8. Add in the rest of the ingredients in the end.
9. Scramble the mixture.
10. Add in the salt and pepper.
11. Boil the ramen noodles according to the instructions on the pack.
12. Drain the noodles and add them into the pan.
13. Mix all the ingredients well and then dish them out.
14. Peel the eggs and place it on the ramen.
15. Garnish the fresh chopped chives on top.
16. Your dish is ready to be served.

2.5 Japanese Miso Ramen with Boiled Eggs Recipe

Preparation Time: 30 minutes

Cooking Time: 10 minutes

Serving: 4

Ingredients:

- Chopped chives, one teaspoon
- Butter, two tablespoon
- Salt, to taste
- Black pepper, to taste
- Miso paste, two teaspoon
- Eggs, four
- Mirin paste, one tablespoon
- Chopped garlic, one teaspoon
- Ramen noodles, four packs

Instructions:
1. Boil the eggs.
2. Make sure to boil the eggs for ten minutes only.

3. Take a large pan.
4. Add the butter and let it meltdown.
5. Add in the miso paste.
6. Mix all the ingredients well.
7. Add the chopped garlic.
8. Add in the rest of the ingredients in the end.
9. Scramble the mixture.
10. Add in the salt and pepper.
11. Boil the ramen noodles according to the instructions on the pack.
12. Drain the noodles and add them into the pan.
13. Mix all the ingredients well and then dish them out.
14. Peel the eggs and place them on the ramen.
15. Garnish the fresh chopped chives on top.
16. Your dish is ready to be served.

2.6 Japanese Bacon, Egg and Cheese Breakfast Ramen Recipe

Preparation Time: 30 minutes

Cooking Time: 10 minutes

Serving: 4

Ingredients:

- Chopped chives, one teaspoon
- Butter, two tablespoon
- Chopped bacon, half pound
- Salt, to taste
- Black pepper, to taste
- Cheese, one cup
- Eggs, four
- Mirin paste, one tablespoon
- Chopped garlic, one teaspoon
- Ramen noodles, four packs

Instructions:

1. Take a large pan.
2. Add the butter and let it meltdown.
3. Add in the chopped bacons.
4. Mix all the ingredients well.
5. Add the chopped garlic.
6. Add in the rest of the ingredients in the end.
7. Scramble the mixture.
8. Add in the salt and pepper.
9. Boil the ramen noodles according to the instructions on the pack.

10. Drain the noodles and add them into the pan.
11. Mix all the ingredients well and then dish them out.
12. Your dish is ready to be served.

2.7 Japanese Ramen with Tofu and Eggs Recipe

Preparation Time: 30 minutes
Cooking Time: 10 minutes
Serving: 4

Ingredients:

- Chopped chives, one teaspoon
- Butter, two tablespoon
- Tofu cubes, half pound
- Salt, to taste
- Black pepper, to taste
- Tamari paste, as required
- Eggs, four
- Mirin paste, one tablespoon
- Chopped garlic, one teaspoon

Instructions:

1. Take a large pan.
2. Add the butter and let it meltdown.
3. Add in the eggs.
4. Add in the tamari paste.
5. Mix the tamari paste and eggs and then add the chopped garlic.
6. Scramble the mixture.
7. Add in the salt and pepper.
8. Add in the tofu cubes and rest of the ingredients in the end.
9. When the eggs are done, dish them out.
10. Add the fresh chopped chives on top.
11. Your dish is ready to be served.

2.8 Japanese Chicken Ramen with Bok Choy and Soy Eggs Recipe

Preparation Time: 30 minutes

Cooking Time: 10 minutes

Serving: 4

Ingredients:

- Onions, half cup
- Rice wine, one tablespoon
- Eggs, four
- Black pepper, to taste
- Salt, to taste
- Cooked chicken, one cup
- Ramen noodles, four packs
- Ginger, one teaspoon
- Bok choy, one cup
- Soy sauce, half cup
- Oil, one tablespoon
- Cilantro, as required

Instructions:

1. Take a large bowl.
2. Add all the ingredients into the bowl.
3. Make the egg mixture.
4. Take a large pan.
5. Heat a pan and then add the oil into the pan.
6. Add the egg mixture on top when the oil heats up.
7. Let the eggs cook from the bottom.
8. Scramble the eggs for ten minutes.
9. Garnish the eggs by adding chopped cilantro on top.
10. Your dish is ready to be served.

2.9 Japanese Egg Tonkotsu Ramen Recipe

Preparation Time: 30 minutes

Cooking Time: 10 minutes

Serving: 4

Ingredients:

- Chopped chives, one teaspoon
- Butter, two tablespoon
- Tonkatsu broth, one cup
- Salt, to taste
- Black pepper, to taste

- Tamari paste, two teaspoon
- Eggs, four
- Mirin paste, one tablespoon
- Chopped garlic, one teaspoon
- Ramen noodles, four packs

Instructions:
1. Take a large pan.
2. Add the butter and let it meltdown.
3. Add in the eggs.
4. Add in the tamari paste.
5. Mix the tamari paste and eggs.
6. Add the chopped garlic.
7. Scramble the mixture.
8. Add in the salt and pepper.
9. Add in the tonkatsu broth and rest of the ingredients in the end.
10. Mix all the ingredients well and then dish them out.
11. Garnish the fresh chopped chives on top.
12. Your dish is ready to be served.

2.10 Japanese Scallops and Egg Ramen Recipe

Preparation Time: 30 minutes

Cooking Time: 10 minutes

Serving: 4

Ingredients:

- Chopped cilantro, one teaspoon
- Butter, two tablespoon
- Chopped scallions, two cups
- Salt, to taste
- Black pepper, to taste
- Tamari paste, two teaspoon
- Eggs, four
- Mirin paste, one tablespoon
- Chopped garlic, one teaspoon
- Ramen noodles, four packs

Instructions:
1. Take a large pan.
2. Add the butter and let it meltdown.
3. Add in the chopped scallions.
4. Add in the tamari paste.
5. Mix all the ingredients well.
6. Add the chopped garlic.
7. Add in the rest of the ingredients in the end.
8. Scramble the mixture.

9. Add in the salt and pepper.
10. Boil the ramen noodles according to the instructions on the pack.
11. Drain the noodles and add them into the pan.
12. Mix all the ingredients well and then dish them out.
13. Garnish the fresh chopped cilantro on top.
14. Your dish is ready to be served.

Chapter 3: The World of Ramen Lunch Recipes

Japanese ramen lunch recipes are full of flavors. There are many varieties of ramen noodles that can be eaten during the lunch time. Following are some easy to make recipes that you can cook today:

3.1 Japanese Ramen Noodle Soup Recipe

Preparation Time: 20 minutes

Cooking Time: 20 minutes

Serving: 4

Ingredients:

- Ramen noodles, two packs
- Miso paste, one teaspoon
- Onion, one cup
- Bell peppers, one cup
- Japanese fresh herbs, half teaspoon
- Water, one cup
- Minced garlic, two tablespoon
- Minced ginger, two tablespoon
- Cilantro, half cup
- Diced carrots, one cup

- Olive oil, two tablespoon
- Water, half cup
- Vegetable stock, two cups
- Chopped tomatoes, one cup

Instructions:
1. Take a pan.
2. Add in the oil and onions.
3. Cook the onions until they become soft and fragrant.
4. Add in the chopped garlic and ginger.
5. Cook the mixture and add the tomatoes into it.
6. Add the spices.
7. Add the miso paste into it when the tomatoes are done.
8. Mix the ingredients carefully and cover the pan.
9. Add the vegetables and rest of the ingredients except the noodles.
10. Let the mixture boil.
11. Add the ramen noodles into the soup mixture.
12. Let the soup cook for ten to fifteen minutes straight.
13. Add cilantro on top.
14. Your dish is ready to be served.

3.2 Japanese Duck Ramen Recipes

Preparation Time: 30 minutes

Cooking Time: 10 minutes

Serving: 4

Ingredients:

- Tomato paste, one cup
- Sliced green onions, half cup
- Mirin paste, one teaspoon
- Cilantro, one cup
- Fresh ginger, one teaspoon
- Miso paste, one tablespoon
- Cooked and shredded duck meat, one cup
- Soy sauce, one tablespoon
- Japanese fresh herbs, half teaspoon
- Fresh shiso leaves, two tablespoon
- Fresh cilantro leaves, half cup
- Chopped tomatoes, half cup
- Ramen, as required

Instructions:
1. Add all the ingredients of the sauce i.e. miso paste, soy sauce, mirin paste and Japanese fresh herbs into a large pan.

2. Add the shredded duck meat, tomato paste, chopped tomatoes and the rest of the ingredients into the mixture.
3. Cook the dish for ten minutes.
4. Add the ramen into the mixture once the sauce is ready.
5. Mix the ramen well.
6. Cook the dish for five minutes.
7. Add the cilantro and the green onions into the dish.
8. Your dish is ready to be served.

3.3 Japanese Sapporo Ramen Recipe

Preparation Time: 30 minutes
Cooking Time: 10 minutes
Serving: 4

Ingredients:

- Bean sprouts, one cup
- Sliced green onions, half cup
- Mirin paste, one teaspoon
- Cilantro, one cup
- Bamboo shoots, one teaspoon
- Miso paste, one tablespoon
- Chashu pork meat, one cup

- Soy sauce, one tablespoon
- Cooking oil, two tablespoon
- Chopped garlic, one teaspoon
- Japanese fresh herbs, half teaspoon
- Fresh shiso leaves, two tablespoon
- Fresh cilantro leaves, half cup
- Dried chili flakes, two teaspoon
- Soft boiled eggs, four
- Ramen, as required

Instructions:
1. Take a large pan.
2. Add the cooking oil and chopped garlic into the pan.
3. Add Chashu pork meat into the pan.
4. Add all the spices into the mixture.
5. Cook the ingredients for five minutes.
6. Add the bean sprouts and ramen into the mixture.
7. Cook all the ingredients well.
8. Peel the soft boiled eggs and add them into the mixture.
9. Cook for five minutes.
10. Garnish the dish with cilantro and green onions.
11. Your dish is ready to be served.

3.4 Japanese Miso Ramen Recipe

Preparation Time: 20 minutes
Cooking Time: 10 minutes
Serving: 4

Ingredients:

- Miso paste, half cup
- Sliced green onions, half cup
- Mirin paste, one teaspoon
- Cilantro, one cup
- Fresh ginger, one teaspoon
- Soy sauce, one tablespoon
- Japanese fresh herbs, half teaspoon
- Fresh shiso leaves, two tablespoon
- Fresh cilantro leaves, half cup
- Minced lemon grass, one teaspoon
- Ramen, as required

Instructions:
1. Heat a large pan.
2. Add the miso paste and the rest of the ingredients into the mixture.
3. Cook the ingredients for ten minutes.

4. Add the ramen into the mixture once the sauce is ready.
5. Mix the ramen well.
6. Cook the dish for five minutes.
7. Add the cilantro into the dish.
8. Your dish is ready to be served.

3.5 Japanese Shoyu Ramen Recipe

Preparation Time: 20 minutes
Cooking Time: 20 minutes
Serving: 4

Ingredients:

- Ramen noodles, two packs
- Spicy chili bean sauce, two teaspoon
- Onion, one cup
- Dashi stock, two cups
- Japanese fresh herbs, half teaspoon
- Water, one cup
- Minced garlic, two tablespoon
- Minced ginger, two tablespoon
- Cilantro, half cup
- Fish cakes, one cup
- Chili oil, two tablespoon

- Shredded nori sheets, half cup
- Sheragi negi, two cups
- Chopped tomatoes, one cup

Instructions:
1. Take a pan.
2. Add in the oil and onions.
3. Cook the onions until they become soft and fragrant.
4. Add in the chopped garlic and ginger.
5. Cook the mixture for a few seconds.
6. Add the spices.
7. Add the sheragi negi into it when the spices are done.
8. Mix the ingredients carefully and cover the pan.
9. Add the fish cakes and rest of the ingredients except the noodles.
10. Let the mixture boil.
11. Add the ramen noodles into the soup mixture.
12. Let the soup cook for ten to fifteen minutes straight.
13. Add shredded nori sheets on top.
14. Your dish is ready to be served.

3.6 Japanese Tantanmen Ramen Recipe

Preparation Time: 30 minutes

Cooking Time: 10 minutes

Serving: 4

Ingredients:

- Minced pork, one cup
- Sliced green onions, half cup
- Tahini paste, one teaspoon
- Cilantro, one cup
- Fresh ginger, one teaspoon
- Oyster sauce, one tablespoon
- Rice wine, three tablespoon
- Soy sauce, one tablespoon
- Japanese fresh herbs, half teaspoon
- Chili oil, two tablespoon
- Fresh cilantro leaves, half cup
- Chopped tomatoes, half cup
- Ramen, as required
- Sesame seeds, half cup
- Bean sprouts, one cup
- Bok choy, one cup

Instructions:

1. Add all the ingredients of the sauce i.e. oyster sauce, soy sauce, rice wine and Japanese fresh herbs into a large pan.
2. Add the vegetables, minced pork, chopped tomatoes and the rest of the ingredients into the mixture.
3. Cook the dish for ten minutes.
4. Add the ramen into the mixture once the sauce is ready.
5. Mix the ramen well.
6. Cook the dish for five minutes.
7. Add the cilantro and the green onions into the dish.
8. Your dish is ready to be served.

3.7 Japanese Spicy Pork Ramen Recipe

Preparation Time: 30 minutes

Cooking Time: 10 minutes

Serving: 4

Ingredients:

- Chili paste, two tablespoon
- Sliced green onions, half cup
- Mirin paste, one teaspoon

- Fresh ginger, one teaspoon
- Miso paste, one tablespoon
- Cooked and shredded pork meat, one cup
- Soy sauce, one tablespoon
- Japanese fresh herbs, half teaspoon
- Fresh shiso leaves, two tablespoon
- Fresh cilantro leaves, half cup
- Chopped tomatoes, half cup
- Ramen, as required

Instructions:
1. Add all the ingredients of the sauce i.e. miso paste, soy sauce, mirin paste and Japanese fresh herbs into a large pan.
2. Add the shredded pork meat, chili paste, chopped tomatoes and the rest of the ingredients into the mixture.
3. Cook the dish for ten minutes.
4. Add the ramen into the mixture once the sauce is ready.
5. Mix the ramen well.
6. Cook the dish for five minutes.
7. Add the green onions into the dish.
8. Your dish is ready to be served.

3.8 Japanese Roast Pork Ramen Recipe

Preparation Time: 30 minutes
Cooking Time: 10 minutes
Serving: 4

Ingredients:

- Shredded nori sheets, two tablespoon
- Sliced green onions, half cup
- Mirin paste, one teaspoon
- Miso paste, one tablespoon
- Roasted and shredded pork meat, one cup
- Soy sauce, one tablespoon
- Japanese fresh herbs, half teaspoon
- Fresh shiso leaves, two tablespoon
- Fresh cilantro leaves, half cup
- Ramen, as required

Instructions:
1. Add all the ingredients of the sauce i.e. miso paste, soy sauce, mirin paste and Japanese fresh herbs into a large pan.
2. Add the roasted pork meat, shiso leaves, chopped tomatoes and the rest of the ingredients into the mixture.

3. Cook the dish for ten minutes.
4. Add the ramen into the mixture once the sauce is ready.
5. Mix the ramen well.
6. Cook the dish for five minutes.
7. Add the shredded nori sheets into the dish.
8. Your dish is ready to be served.

3.9 Japanese Chargrilled Chicken Ramen Recipe

Preparation Time: 30 minutes

Cooking Time: 20 minutes

Serving: 4

Ingredients:

- Chicken stock, two cups
- Crushed garlic, two
- Chicken pieces, one pound
- Salt, to taste
- Black pepper, to taste
- Olive oil, two tablespoon
- Dried white wine, one cup
- Onion, one cup
- All-purpose flour, three tablespoon
- Worcestershire sauce, two

tablespoon
- Softened butter, three tablespoon
- Bay leaf, one
- Fresh thyme, two tablespoon
- Grated or sliced cheese, one cup
- Chopped cilantro, one cup
- Ramen noodles, four packs

Instructions:
1. Take a large skillet.
2. Add the oil and onions into the skillet.
3. Cook the onions until they turn golden brown.
4. Add the crushed garlic into the skillet.
5. Add the spices into the mixture.
6. Add all-purpose flour, Worcestershire sauce and dried white wine.
7. Add the butter and then add the chicken stock and ramen noodles.
8. Grill the chicken pieces over a grill pan.
9. Cut the chicken into long pieces.
10. Add the chicken into the ramen mixture.
11. The dish is ready to be served.

3.10 Japanese Lemongrass, Chicken and Ginger Ramen Recipe

Preparation Time: 30 minutes

Cooking Time: 10 minutes

Serving: 4

Ingredients:

- Tomato paste, one cup
- Sliced green onions, half cup
- Mirin paste, one teaspoon
- Cilantro, one cup
- Dried lemongrass, two teaspoon
- Fresh ginger slices, half cup
- Miso paste, one tablespoon
- Cooked and shredded chicken meat, one cup
- Soy sauce, one tablespoon
- Japanese fresh herbs, half teaspoon
- Fresh shiso leaves, two tablespoon
- Lemon juice, half cup
- Fresh cilantro leaves, half cup
- Chopped tomatoes, half cup
- Ramen, as required

Instructions:

1. Add all the ingredients of the sauce i.e. miso paste, soy sauce, mirin paste and Japanese fresh herbs into a large pan.
2. Add the shredded chicken meat, lemongrass, ginger slices, tomato paste, chopped tomatoes and the rest of the ingredients into the mixture.
3. Cook the dish for ten minutes.
4. Add the ramen into the mixture once the sauce is ready.
5. Mix the ramen well.
6. Cook the dish for five minutes.
7. Add the cilantro and the green onions into the dish.
8. Your dish is ready to be served.

3.11 Japanese Spicy Beef Ramen Recipe

Preparation Time: 30 minutes

Cooking Time: 10 minutes

Serving: 4

Ingredients:

- Chili paste, two tablespoon
- Sliced green onions, half cup
- Mirin paste, one teaspoon

- Fresh ginger, one teaspoon
- Miso paste, one tablespoon
- Cooked and shredded beef meat, one cup
- Soy sauce, one tablespoon
- Chopped garlic, one teaspoon
- Japanese fresh herbs, half teaspoon
- Fresh shiso leaves, two tablespoon
- Fresh cilantro leaves, half cup
- Chopped tomatoes, half cup
- Ramen, as required

Instructions:
1. Add all the ingredients of the sauce i.e. miso paste, soy sauce, mirin paste and Japanese fresh herbs into a large pan.
2. Add the shredded beef meat, chili paste, chopped tomatoes and the rest of the ingredients into the mixture.
3. Cook the dish for ten minutes.
4. Add the ramen into the mixture once the sauce is ready.
5. Mix the ramen well.
6. Cook the dish for five minutes.
7. Add the green onions into the dish.
8. Your dish is ready to be served.

3.12 Japanese Prawn Ramen Recipe

Preparation Time: 20 minutes
Cooking Time: 20 minutes
Serving: 4

Ingredients:

- Ramen noodles, two packs
- Miso paste, one teaspoon
- Onion, one cup
- Prawns, one pound
- Bell peppers, one cup
- Japanese fresh herbs, half teaspoon
- Water, one cup
- Minced garlic, two tablespoon
- Minced ginger, two tablespoon
- Cilantro, half cup
- Diced carrots, one cup
- Olive oil, two tablespoon
- Water, half cup
- Vegetable stock, two cups
- Chopped tomatoes, one cup

Instructions:
1. Take a pan.
2. Add in the oil and onions.
3. Cook the onions until they become soft and fragrant.
4. Add in the chopped garlic and ginger.
5. Cook the mixture and add the tomatoes into it.
6. Add the spices.
7. Add the miso paste into it when the tomatoes are done.
8. Mix the ingredients carefully and cover the pan.
9. Add the prawns, vegetables and rest of the ingredients except the noodles.
10. Let the mixture boil.
11. Add the ramen noodles into the soup mixture.
12. Let the soup cook for ten to fifteen minutes straight.
13. Add cilantro on top.
14. Your dish is ready to be served.

3.13 Japanese Ramen Noodle Salad Recipe

Preparation Time: 20 minutes
Cooking Time: 40 minutes
Serving: 2

Ingredients:
- Ginger powder, one tablespoon
- Chicken shredded, two cups
- Garlic powder, two teaspoon
- Maple syrup, half teaspoon
- Sesame oil, one teaspoon
- Soy sauce, one teaspoon
- Sriracha, one tablespoon
- Lime juice, one tablespoon
- Salt, to taste
- Ramen noodles, four packs
- Pepper, to taste

Instructions:
1. Boil the ramen noodles in a large pot full of water.
2. Drain the noodles when they are cooked.
3. Take a large bowl and add boiled noodles into it.
4. Add the ginger and garlic powder.
5. Mix well so that everything mixes well.

6. Add lime juice, maple syrup, cooked shredded chicken, Japanese red chili and soy sauce.
7. Add the salt and pepper as you like.
8. Add the sesame oil and mix well so that a homogeneous mixture is obtained.
9. Add the sriracha into the mixture.
10. Mix everything well.
11. The salad is ready to be served.

3.14 Japanese Mongolian Beef Ramen Recipe

Preparation Time: 30 minutes
Cooking Time: 10 minutes
Serving: 4

Ingredients:

- Nori paste, two tablespoon
- Sliced green onions, half cup
- Mirin paste, one teaspoon
- Fresh ginger, one teaspoon
- Miso paste, one tablespoon
- Beef meat pieces, one cup
- Soy sauce, one tablespoon
- Mongolian spice, two tablespoon
- Olive oil, two teaspoon

- Chopped garlic, one teaspoon
- Japanese fresh herbs, half teaspoon
- Fresh shiso leaves, two tablespoon
- Fresh cilantro leaves, half cup
- Chopped tomatoes, half cup
- Ramen, as required

Instructions:
1. Add the beef pieces into a pan.
2. Add the Mongolian spice and olive oil into the pan.
3. Cook the beef pieces for ten minutes or until they are completely cooked.
4. Dish out the beef pieces and shred them when cooled.
5. Take a large sauce pan.
6. Add all the ingredients of the sauce into the pan.
7. Add the shredded beef meat, nori paste, chopped tomatoes and the rest of the ingredients into the mixture.
8. Cook the dish for ten minutes.
9. Add the ramen into the mixture once the sauce is ready.
10. Mix the ramen well.
11. Cook the dish for five minutes.
12. Add the green onions into the dish.
13. Your dish is ready to be served.

3.15 Japanese Meatball Ramen Recipe

Preparation Time: 30 minutes
Cooking Time: 20 minutes
Serving: 4

Ingredients:

- Beef stock, two cups
- Crushed garlic, two
- Frozen bacon and beef meatballs, one pound
- Salt, to taste
- Black pepper, to taste
- Olive oil, two tablespoon
- Dried white wine, one cup
- Onion, one cup
- All-purpose flour, three tablespoon
- Worcestershire sauce, two tablespoon
- Softened butter, three tablespoon
- Bay leaf, one
- Fresh thyme, two tablespoon
- Grated or sliced cheese, one cup
- Chopped cilantro, one cup
- Ramen noodles, four packs

Instructions:
1. Take a large skillet.
2. Add the oil and onions into the skillet.
3. Cook the onions until they turn golden brown.
4. Add the crushed garlic into the skillet.
5. Add the spices into the mixture.
6. Add the all-purpose flour, Worcestershire sauce and dried white wine.
7. Add the butter and then add the beef stock and ramen noodles.
8. Fry the frozen meatballs in a pan full of cooking oil.
9. Dish out the meatballs when they turn golden brown on all sides.
10. Add the fried meatballs into the ramen mixture.
11. The dish is ready to be served.

3.16 Japanese Ramen Noodle Skillet with Steak Recipe

Preparation Time: 30 minutes

Cooking Time: 20 minutes

Serving: 4

Ingredients:

- Chicken stock, two cups
- Crushed garlic, two
- Steak meat, one pound
- Salt, to taste
- Black pepper, to taste
- Olive oil, two tablespoon
- Dried white wine, one cup
- Onion, one cup
- All-purpose flour, three tablespoon
- Worcestershire sauce, two tablespoon
- Softened butter, three tablespoon
- Bay leaf, one
- Fresh thyme, two tablespoon
- Grated or sliced cheese, one cup
- Chopped cilantro, one cup
- Ramen noodles, four packs

Instructions:

1. Take a large skillet.
2. Add the oil and onions into the skillet.
3. Cook the onions until they turn golden brown.
4. Add the crushed garlic into the skillet.
5. Add the spices into the mixture.
6. Add all-purpose flour, Worcestershire sauce and dried white wine.
7. Add the butter and then add the chicken stock and ramen noodles.
8. Grill the steak meat over a grill pan.
9. Cut the steak into long pieces.
10. Add the steak pieces on top of the ramen mixture.
11. Garnish the noodles with chopped cilantro.
12. The dish is ready to be served.

3.17 Japanese Cheese Ramen Recipe

Preparation Time: 30 minutes
Cooking Time: 20 minutes
Serving: 4

Ingredients:

- Mushroom sauce, one cup
- Miso paste, one teaspoon
- Onion, one cup

- Ramen noodles, four cups
- Shredded mozzarella cheese, one cup
- Water, one cup
- Bok choy, one cup
- Rice vinegar, one tablespoon
- Minced garlic, two tablespoon
- Minced ginger, two tablespoon
- Cilantro leaves, half cup
- Olive oil, two tablespoon
- Water, half cup
- Vegetable stock, half cup
- Chopped tomatoes, one cup

Instructions:
1. Take a pan.
2. Add in the oil and onions.
3. Cook the onions until they become soft and fragrant.
4. Add in the chopped garlic and ginger.
5. Cook the mixture and add the tomatoes into it.
6. Add the spices.
7. When the tomatoes are done, add the miso paste into it.
8. Mix the ingredients carefully and cover the pan.
9. Add the bok choy and rest of the ingredients.

10. Add the water into the mixture and let the mixture boil.
11. Add the ramen noodles into the mixture.
12. Let the noodles cook for ten to fifteen minutes straight.
13. Add cilantro leaves and shredded cheese on top.
14. Your dish is ready to be served.

3.18 Japanese Ramen Burger Recipe

Preparation Time: 20 minutes
Cooking Time: 20 minutes
Serving: 4

Ingredients:

- Ramen buns, as required
- Minced beef meat, one cup
- Bread crumbs, one cup
- Egg, one
- Chopped parsley, half cup
- Fresh chopped cilantro, half cup
- Salt, to taste
- Black pepper, to taste
- Olive oil, for frying
- Yoghurt, half cup

- Lemon juice, a quarter cup
- Fresh chopped cilantro, two tablespoon
- Butter, one tablespoon

Instructions:

1. Take a large bowl.
2. Add the beef meat, salt, pepper, bread crumbs and egg into it.
3. Mix all the ingredients well.
4. Add the chopped cilantro and parsley into the mixture.
5. Mix the ingredients until they become smooth.
6. Shape the mixture into patties.
7. Add the olive oil in a large pan and cook the patties.
8. Cook the patties until they turn golden brown from both sides.
9. In the meanwhile, in a small bowl, add the yoghurt, lemon juice and fresh cilantro.
10. Mix it to form a paste.
11. Add butter on the ramen and heat them.
12. Add the beef patty on the ramen.
13. Add the paste on top of the patty and cover it with the ramen bun.
14. The ramen burger is ready to be served.

3.19 Japanese Garlic and Shrimp Ramen Recipe

Preparation Time: 20 minutes
Cooking Time: 20 minutes
Serving: 4

Ingredients:

- Ramen noodles, two packs
- Miso paste, one teaspoon
- Onion, one cup
- Shrimps, one pound
- Bell peppers, one cup
- Japanese fresh herbs, half teaspoon
- Water, one cup
- Minced garlic, two tablespoon
- Minced ginger, two tablespoon
- Cilantro, half cup
- Diced carrots, one cup
- Olive oil, two tablespoon
- Water, half cup
- Vegetable stock, two cups
- Chopped tomatoes, one cup

Instructions:

1. Take a pan.
2. Add in the oil and onions.
3. Cook the onions until they become soft and fragrant.
4. Add in the chopped garlic and ginger.
5. Cook the mixture and add the tomatoes into it.
6. Add the spices.
7. Add the miso paste into it when the tomatoes are done.
8. Mix the ingredients carefully and cover the pan.
9. Add the shrimps, vegetables and rest of the ingredients except the noodles.
10. Let the mixture boil.
11. Add the ramen noodles into the soup mixture.
12. Let the soup cook for ten to fifteen minutes straight.
13. Add cilantro on top.
14. Your dish is ready to be served.

3.20 Japanese Beef and Ramen Stir-Fry Recipe

Preparation Time: 30 minutes

Cooking Time: 10 minutes

Serving: 4

Ingredients:

- Ramen noodles, four packs
- Sesame oil, one tablespoon
- Cilantro, one cup
- Sesame seeds, half cup
- Fresh ginger, one teaspoon
- Dark soy sauce, one tablespoon
- Mirin paste, one tablespoon
- Dried shisho leaves, half teaspoon
- Chili garlic sauce, two tablespoon
- Thyme, one tablespoon
- Lemon zest, one teaspoon
- Lemon juice, half cup
- Beef pieces, one pound
- Fresh chopped garlic, half cup
- Fresh basil leaves, a quarter cup
- Vegetable broth, one cup

Instructions:
1. Boil the ramen noodles.
2. Add all the ingredients of the sauce into a wok.
3. Cook the ingredients.
4. Add the beef pieces, lemon juice, thyme, lemon zest and rest of the ingredients into the mixture.

5. Add the ramen noodles into the mixture once the mixture is ready.
6. Mix the ramen noodles well and cook it for five minutes.
7. Add the cilantro into the dish.
8. Your dish is ready to be served.

Chapter 4: The World of Ramen Dinner Recipes

Ramen dinner recipes are well- known all over the world for its mesmerizing flavors and varieties. Following are some amazing and healthy Ramen dinner recipes that you would love to make at home:

4.1 Japanese Parmesan and Garlic Ramen Recipe

Preparation Time: 20 minutes

Cooking Time: 20 minutes

Serving: 4

Ingredients:

- Parmesan cheese, one cup
- Ramen noodles, two packs
- Miso paste, one teaspoon
- Onion, one cup
- Bell peppers, one cup
- Japanese fresh herbs, half teaspoon
- Water, one cup
- Minced garlic, two tablespoon
- Cilantro, half cup
- Diced carrots, one cup

- Olive oil, two tablespoon
- Water, half cup
- Vegetable stock, two cups
- Chopped tomatoes, one cup

Instructions:
1. Take a pan.
2. Add in the oil and onions.
3. Cook the onions until they become soft and fragrant.
4. Add in the chopped garlic.
5. Cook the mixture and add the tomatoes into it.
6. Add the spices.
7. Add the miso paste into it when the tomatoes are done.
8. Mix the ingredients carefully and cover the pan.
9. Add the vegetables and rest of the ingredients except the noodles and parmesan cheese.
10. Let the mixture boil.
11. Add the ramen noodles into the soup mixture.
12. Let the soup cook for ten to fifteen minutes straight.
13. Add cilantro and parmesan cheese on top.
14. Your dish is ready to be served.

4.2 Japanese Ginger and Beef Stir-Fry Ramen Recipe

Preparation Time: 30 minutes
Cooking Time: 10 minutes
Serving: 4

Ingredients:

- Ramen noodles, four packs
- Sesame oil, one tablespoon
- Cilantro, one cup
- Sesame seeds, half cup
- Fresh ginger, two tablespoon
- Dark soy sauce, one tablespoon
- Mirin paste, one tablespoon
- Dried shisho leaves, half teaspoon
- Chili garlic sauce, two tablespoon
- Thyme, one tablespoon
- Lemon zest, one teaspoon
- Lemon juice, half cup
- Beef pieces, one pound
- Fresh basil leaves, a quarter cup
- Vegetable broth, one cup

Instructions:

1. Boil the ramen noodles.
2. Add all the ingredients of the sauce into a wok.
3. Cook the ingredients.
4. Add the beef pieces, chopped ginger, lemon juice, thyme, lemon zest and rest of the ingredients into the mixture.
5. Add the ramen noodles into the mixture once the mixture is ready.
6. Mix the ramen noodles well and cook it for five minutes.
7. Add the cilantro into the dish.
8. Your dish is ready to be served.

4.3 Japanese Peanut and Chicken Ramen Recipe

Preparation Time: 30 minutes
Cooking Time: 20 minutes
Serving: 4

Ingredients:

- Mushroom sauce, one cup
- Miso paste, one teaspoon
- Onion, one cup
- Ramen noodles, four cups
- Peanuts, one cup

- Water, one cup
- Chicken pieces, one cup
- Rice vinegar, one tablespoon
- Minced garlic, two tablespoon
- Minced ginger, two tablespoon
- Cilantro leaves, half cup
- Olive oil, two tablespoon
- Water, half cup
- Chicken stock, half cup
- Chopped tomatoes, one cup

Instructions:
1. Take a pan.
2. Add in the oil and onions.
3. Cook the onions until they become soft and fragrant.
4. Add in the chopped garlic and ginger.
5. Cook the mixture and add the tomatoes into it.
6. Add the spices.
7. When the tomatoes are done, add the chicken stock, and miso paste into it.
8. Mix the ingredients carefully and cover the pan.
9. Add the chicken and rest of the ingredients.
10. Add the water into the mixture and let the mixture boil.
11. Add the ramen noodles into the mixture.

12. Let the soup cook for ten to fifteen minutes straight.
13. Add cilantro leaves and peanuts on top.
14. Your dish is ready to be served.

4.4 Japanese Roasted Chicken Ramen Recipe

Preparation Time: 30 minutes

Cooking Time: 20 minutes

Serving: 4

Ingredients:

- Chicken stock, two cups
- Crushed garlic, two
- Chicken pieces, one pound
- Salt, to taste
- Black pepper, to taste
- Olive oil, two tablespoon
- Dried white wine, one cup
- Onion, one cup
- All-purpose flour, three tablespoon
- Worcestershire sauce, two tablespoon
- Softened butter, three tablespoon
- Bay leaf, one

- Fresh thyme, two tablespoon
- Grated or sliced cheese, one cup
- Chopped cilantro, one cup
- Ramen noodles, four packs

Instructions:
1. Take a large skillet.
2. Add the oil and onions into the skillet.
3. Cook the onions until they turn golden brown.
4. Add the crushed garlic into the skillet.
5. Add the spices into the mixture.
6. Add the all-purpose flour, Worcestershire sauce and dried white wine.
7. Add the butter and then add the chicken stock and ramen noodles.
8. Roast the chicken pieces in a preheated oven.
9. Cut the chicken into long pieces.
10. Add the chicken into the ramen mixture.
11. The dish is ready to be served.

4.5 Japanese Sirarcha and Shrimp Ramen Recipe

Preparation Time: 20 minutes
Cooking Time: 20 minutes
Serving: 4

Ingredients:

- Ramen noodles, two packs
- Miso paste, one teaspoon
- Onion, one cup
- Shrimps, one pound
- Bell peppers, one cup
- Japanese fresh herbs, half teaspoon
- Water, one cup
- Minced garlic, two tablespoon
- Minced ginger, two tablespoon
- Cilantro, half cup
- Diced carrots, one cup
- Olive oil, two tablespoon
- Sirarcha sauce, half cup
- Fish stock, two cups
- Chopped tomatoes, one cup

Instructions:
1. Take a pan.
2. Add in the oil and onions.
3. Cook the onions until they become soft and fragrant.
4. Add in the chopped garlic and ginger.
5. Cook the mixture and add the tomatoes into it.
6. Add the spices.
7. Add the miso paste and sirarcha into it when the tomatoes are done.
8. Mix the ingredients carefully and cover the pan.
9. Add the shrimps, vegetables and rest of the ingredients except the noodles.
10. Let the mixture boil.
11. Add the ramen noodles into the soup mixture.
12. Let the soup cook for ten to fifteen minutes straight.
13. Add cilantro on top.
14. Your dish is ready to be served.

4.6 Japanese Bacon Ramen Soup Recipe

Preparation Time: 20 minutes
Cooking Time: 20 minutes
Serving: 4

Ingredients:

- Ramen noodles, two packs
- Miso paste, one teaspoon
- Onion, one cup
- Chopped bacon, one cup
- Japanese fresh herbs, half teaspoon
- Water, one cup
- Minced garlic, two tablespoon
- Minced ginger, two tablespoon
- Cilantro, half cup
- Olive oil, two tablespoon
- Water, half cup
- Chicken stock, two cups
- Chopped tomatoes, one cup

Instructions:
1. Take a pan.

2. Add in the oil and onions.
3. Cook the onions until they become soft and fragrant.
4. Add in the chopped garlic and ginger.
5. Cook the mixture and add the tomatoes into it.
6. Add the spices.
7. Add the chopped bacon into it when the tomatoes are done.
8. Mix the ingredients carefully and cover the pan.
9. Add the rest of the ingredients except the noodles.
10. Let the mixture boil.
11. Add the ramen noodles into the soup mixture.
12. Let the soup cook for ten to fifteen minutes straight.
13. Add cilantro on top.
14. Your dish is ready to be served.

4.7 Japanese Sweet and Sour Pork Ramen Recipe

Preparation Time: 30 minutes
Cooking Time: 10 minutes
Serving: 4

Ingredients:

- Sweet and sour sauce, one cup
- Chili paste, two tablespoon
- Sliced green onions, half cup
- Mirin paste, one teaspoon
- Fresh ginger, one teaspoon
- Miso paste, one tablespoon
- Cooked and shredded pork meat, one cup
- Soy sauce, one tablespoon
- Japanese fresh herbs, half teaspoon
- Fresh shiso leaves, two tablespoon
- Fresh cilantro leaves, half cup
- Chopped tomatoes, half cup
- Ramen, as required

Instructions:

1. Add all the ingredients of the sauce i.e. miso paste, soy sauce, mirin paste and Japanese fresh herbs into a large pan.
2. Add the shredded pork meat, sweet and sour sauce, chopped tomatoes and the rest of the ingredients into the mixture.
3. Cook the dish for ten minutes.
4. Add the ramen into the mixture once the sauce is ready.
5. Mix the ramen well.
6. Cook the dish for five minutes.
7. Add the green onions into the dish.
8. Your dish is ready to be served.

4.8 Japanese Cheesy Tuna Ramen Recipe

Preparation Time: 30 minutes
Cooking Time: 20 minutes
Serving: 4

Ingredients:

- Miso paste, one teaspoon
- Onion, one cup
- Ramen noodles, four cups
- Shredded mozzarella cheese, one cup
- Water, one cup
- Tuna pieces, one cup

- Rice vinegar, one tablespoon
- Minced garlic, two tablespoon
- Minced ginger, two tablespoon
- Cilantro leaves, half cup
- Olive oil, two tablespoon
- Water, half cup
- Fish stock, half cup
- Chopped tomatoes, one cup

Instructions:
1. Take a pan.
2. Add in the oil and onions.
3. Cook the onions until they become soft and fragrant.
4. Add in the chopped garlic and ginger.
5. Cook the mixture and add the tomatoes into it.
6. Add the spices.
7. When the tomatoes are done, add the miso paste into it.
8. Mix the ingredients carefully and cover the pan.
9. Add the tuna pieces and rest of the ingredients.
10. Add the water into the mixture and let the mixture boil.
11. Add the ramen noodles into the mixture.
12. Let the noodles cook for ten to fifteen minutes straight.

13. Add cilantro leaves and shredded cheese on top.
14. Your dish is ready to be served.

4.9 Japanese Ramen and Tomato Soup Recipe

Preparation Time: 30 minutes
Cooking Time: 10 minutes
Serving: 4

Ingredients:

- Tomato paste, one cup
- Sliced green onions, half cup
- Mirin paste, one teaspoon
- Cilantro, one cup
- Fresh ginger, one teaspoon
- Miso paste, one tablespoon
- Soy sauce, one tablespoon
- Japanese fresh herbs, half teaspoon
- Fresh shiso leaves, two tablespoon
- Fresh cilantro leaves, half cup
- Chopped tomatoes, half cup
- Ramen, as required

Instructions:

1. Add all the ingredients of the sauce i.e. miso paste, soy sauce, mirin paste and Japanese fresh herbs into a large pan.
2. Add the tomato paste, chopped tomatoes and the rest of the ingredients into the mixture.
3. Cook the dish for ten minutes.
4. Add the ramen into the mixture once the sauce is ready.
5. Mix the ramen well.
6. Cook the dish for five minutes.
7. Add the cilantro and the green onions into the dish.
8. Your dish is ready to be served.

4.10 Japanese Chili Ramen Recipe

Preparation Time: 20 minutes
Cooking Time: 20 minutes
Serving: 4

Ingredients:

- Ramen noodles, two packs
- Miso paste, one teaspoon
- Onion, one cup
- Chili paste, one tablespoon
- Japanese fresh herbs, half teaspoon

- Water, one cup
- Minced garlic, two tablespoon
- Cilantro, half cup
- Chopped green chilies, one cup
- Olive oil, two tablespoon
- Vegetable stock, two cups
- Chopped tomatoes, one cup

Instructions:
1. Take a pan.
2. Add in the oil and onions.
3. Cook the onions until they become soft and fragrant.
4. Add in the chopped garlic.
5. Cook the mixture and add the tomatoes into it.
6. Add the spices.
7. Add the chili paste into it when the tomatoes are done.
8. Mix the ingredients carefully and cover the pan.
9. Add the chopped green chilies and rest of the ingredients except the noodles.
10. Let the mixture boil.
11. Add the ramen noodles into the mixture.
12. Let the ingredients cook for ten to fifteen minutes straight.
13. Add cilantro on top.
14. Your dish is ready to be served.

4.11 Japanese Chicken and Mushroom Ramen Recipe

Preparation Time: 20 minutes

Cooking Time: 20 minutes

Serving: 4

Ingredients:

- Ramen noodles, two packs
- Miso paste, one teaspoon
- Onion, one cup
- Chicken pieces, one cup
- Japanese fresh herbs, half teaspoon
- Water, one cup
- Minced garlic, two tablespoon
- Cilantro, half cup
- Sliced mushrooms, one cup
- Olive oil, two tablespoon
- Water, half cup
- Chicken stock, two cups
- Chopped tomatoes, one cup

Instructions:
1. Take a pan.
2. Add in the oil and onions.
3. Cook the onions until they become soft and fragrant.
4. Add in the chopped garlic.
5. Cook the mixture and add the tomatoes into it.
6. Add the spices.
7. Add the chicken pieces into it when the tomatoes are done.
8. Mix the ingredients carefully and cover the pan.
9. Add the mushrooms and rest of the ingredients except the noodles.
10. Let the mixture boil.
11. Add the ramen noodles into the soup mixture.
12. Let the soup cook for ten to fifteen minutes straight.
13. Add cilantro on top.
14. Your dish is ready to be served.

4.12 Japanese Parmesan Chicken Ramen Recipe

Preparation Time: 20 minutes

Cooking Time: 20 minutes

Serving: 4

Ingredients:

- Parmesan cheese, one cup
- Ramen noodles, two packs
- Miso paste, one teaspoon
- Onion, one cup
- Chicken pieces, one cup
- Japanese fresh herbs, half teaspoon
- Water, one cup
- Minced garlic, two tablespoon
- Cilantro, half cup
- Olive oil, two tablespoon
- Water, half cup
- Chicken stock, two cups
- Chopped tomatoes, one cup

Instructions:
1. Take a pan.
2. Add in the oil and onions.
3. Cook the onions until they become soft and fragrant.
4. Add in the chopped garlic.
5. Cook the mixture and add the tomatoes into it.
6. Add the spices.
7. Add the miso paste into it when the tomatoes are done.

8. Add the chicken pieces and rest of the ingredients except the noodles and parmesan cheese.
9. Let the mixture boil.
10. Add the ramen noodles into the soup mixture.
11. Let the soup cook for ten to fifteen minutes straight.
12. Add cilantro and parmesan cheese on top.
13. Your dish is ready to be served.

4.13 Japanese Chicken Lo Mein Ramen Recipe

Preparation Time: 30 minutes

Cooking Time: 10 minutes

Serving: 4

Ingredients:

- Diced cabbage, one cup
- Brown sugar, two tablespoon
- Sliced green onions, half cup
- Mirin paste, one teaspoon
- Fresh ginger, one teaspoon
- Miso paste, one tablespoon
- Cooked and shredded chicken meat, one cup

- Soy sauce, one tablespoon
- Shiitake mushrooms, one cup
- Japanese fresh herbs, half teaspoon
- Fresh shiso leaves, two tablespoon
- Fresh cilantro leaves, half cup
- Chopped tomatoes, half cup
- Ramen, as required

Instructions:
1. Add all the ingredients of the sauce i.e. miso paste, soy sauce, mirin paste and Japanese fresh herbs into a large pan.
2. Add the shredded chicken, diced cabbage, brown sugar, shitake mushrooms and the rest of the ingredients into the mixture.
3. Cook the dish for ten minutes.
4. Add the ramen into the mixture once the sauce is ready.
5. Mix the ramen well.
6. Cook the dish for five minutes.
7. Add the green onions into the dish.
8. Your dish is ready to be served.

4.14 Japanese Shrimp Ramen Recipe

Preparation Time: 30 minutes
Cooking Time: 10 minutes

Serving: 4

Ingredients:

- Shiitake mushrooms, one cup
- Diced carrots, one cup
- Sliced green onions, half cup
- Mirin paste, one teaspoon
- Fresh ginger, one teaspoon
- Miso paste, one tablespoon
- Devilled shrimps, one cup
- Soy sauce, one tablespoon
- Chopped garlic, one teaspoon
- Japanese fresh herbs, half teaspoon
- Fresh shiso leaves, two tablespoon
- Fresh cilantro leaves, half cup
- Chopped tomatoes, half cup
- Ramen, as required

Instructions:
1. Add all the ingredients of the sauce i.e. miso paste, soy sauce, mirin paste and Japanese fresh herbs into a large pan.

2. Add the devilled shrimps, carrots, mushrooms, chopped tomatoes and the rest of the ingredients into the mixture.
3. Cook the dish for ten minutes.
4. Add the ramen into the mixture once the sauce is ready.
5. Mix the ramen well.
6. Cook the dish for five minutes.
7. Add the green onions into the dish.
8. Your dish is ready to be served.

4.15 Japanese Green Pepper and Chicken Ramen Recipe

Preparation Time: 20 minutes

Cooking Time: 20 minutes

Serving: 4

Ingredients:

- Ramen noodles, two packs
- Miso paste, one teaspoon
- Onion, one cup
- Chicken pieces, one cup
- Japanese fresh herbs, half teaspoon
- Water, one cup
- Minced garlic, two tablespoon

- Cilantro, half cup
- Green pepper, one cup
- Olive oil, two tablespoon
- Water, half cup
- Chicken stock, two cups
- Chopped tomatoes, one cup

Instructions:
1. Take a pan.
2. Add in the oil and onions.
3. Cook the onions until they become soft and fragrant.
4. Add in the chopped garlic.
5. Cook the mixture and add the tomatoes into it.
6. Add the spices.
7. Add the chicken pieces into it when the tomatoes are done.
8. Mix the ingredients carefully and cover the pan.
9. Add the green pepper and rest of the ingredients except the noodles.
10. Let the mixture boil.
11. Add the ramen noodles into the soup mixture.
12. Let the soup cook for ten to fifteen minutes straight.
13. Add cilantro on top.
14. Your dish is ready to be served.

4.16 Japanese Creamy Tonkotsu Ramen Recipe

Preparation time: 30 minutes
Cooking Time: 10 minutes
Serving: 4

Ingredients:

- Heavy cream, one cup
- Sliced green onions, half cup
- Mirin paste, one teaspoon
- Cilantro, one cup
- Fresh ginger, one teaspoon
- Miso paste, one tablespoon
- Soy sauce, one tablespoon
- Japanese fresh herbs, half teaspoon
- Chopped leeks, two tablespoon
- Chicken meat, one cup
- Tonkatsu broth, one cup
- Fresh cilantro leaves, half cup
- Minced lemon grass, one teaspoon
- Ramen, as required

Instructions:

1. Add all the ingredients of the sauce i.e. miso paste, soy sauce, mirin paste and Japanese fresh herbs into a large pan.
2. Add the heavy cream and the rest of the ingredients into the mixture.
3. Cook the dish for ten minutes.
4. Add the ramen into the mixture once the sauce is ready.
5. Mix the ramen well.
6. Close the lid of the instant pot.
7. Cook the dish for five more minutes.
8. Add the cilantro into the dish.
9. Your dish is ready to be served.

4.17 Japanese Miso and Crispy Pork Ramen Recipe

Preparation Time: 20 minutes

Cooking Time: 10 minutes

Serving: 4

Ingredients:

- Miso paste, half cup
- Sliced green onions, half cup
- Mirin paste, one teaspoon
- Cilantro, one cup

- Fresh ginger, one teaspoon
- Soy sauce, one tablespoon
- Japanese fresh herbs, half teaspoon
- Fresh shiso leaves, two tablespoon
- Fresh cilantro leaves, half cup
- Minced lemon grass, one teaspoon
- Ramen, as required
- Pork strips, one cup
- Corn starch, two teaspoon
- Cooking oil, as required

Instructions:
1. Heat a large pan.
2. Add the cooking oil and let it heat.
3. Mix the pork and cornstarch and add it into the heated oil.
4. Cook the pork well for about five minutes.
5. Dish out the pork strips and set aside when done.
6. Add the miso paste and the rest of the ingredients into the mixture.
7. Cook the ingredients for ten minutes.
8. Add the ramen into the mixture once the sauce is ready.
9. Mix the ramen well.
10. Cook the dish for five minutes.
11. Add the crispy pork on top.

12. Add the cilantro into the dish.
13. Your dish is ready to be served.

4.18 Japanese Shio and Pork Ramen Recipe

Preparation Time: 20 minutes
Cooking Time: 20 minutes
Serving: 4

Ingredients:

- Ramen noodles, two packs
- Cooked and shredded pork, one cup
- Spicy chili bean sauce, two teaspoon
- Onion, one cup
- Dashi stock, two cups
- Japanese fresh herbs, half teaspoon
- Water, one cup
- Minced garlic, two tablespoon
- Minced ginger, two tablespoon
- Cilantro, half cup
- Chili oil, two tablespoon
- Shredded nori sheets, half cup
- Sheragi negi, two cups
- Chopped tomatoes, one cup

Instructions:
1. Take a pan.
2. Add in the oil and onions.
3. Cook the onions until they become soft and fragrant.
4. Add in the chopped garlic and ginger.
5. Cook the mixture for a few seconds.
6. Add the spices.
7. Add the sgeragi negi and shredded pork into it when the spices are done.
8. Mix the ingredients carefully and cover the pan.
9. Let the mixture boil.
10. Add the ramen noodles into the soup mixture.
11. Let the soup cook for ten to fifteen minutes straight.
12. Add shredded nori sheets on top.
13. Your dish is ready to be served.

4.19 Japanese Ramen Noodle Coleslaw Recipe

Preparation Time: 20 minutes
Cooking Time: 40 minutes
Serving: 2

Ingredients:

- Coleslaw mix, two cups
- Maple syrup, half teaspoon
- Sesame oil, one teaspoon
- Soy sauce, one teaspoon
- Salt, to taste
- Ramen noodles, four packs
- Pepper, to taste

Instructions:
1. Boil the ramen noodles in a large pot full of water.
2. Drain the noodles when they are cooked.
3. Take a large bowl and add boiled noodles into it.
4. Add the rest of the ingredients into the bowl.
5. Add the salt and pepper as you like.
6. Add the sesame oil and mix well so that a consistent mixture is obtained.
7. The salad is ready to be served.

4.20 Japanese Instant Ramen Noodle Recipe

Preparation Time: 10 minutes
Cooking Time: 10 minutes
Serving: 4

Ingredients:

- Water, two cups
- Ramen noodles, two pack
- Mirin paste, one tablespoon
- Mix spice, half cup
- Dashi powder, two tablespoon
- Fresh shiso leaves, a quarter cup
- Sesame oil, one tablespoon

Instructions:
1. Take a large pan.
2. Add all the ingredients into the pan.
3. Cook the ingredients for ten minutes.
4. Garnish it with shiso leaves.
5. Your dish is ready to be served.

Chapter 5: The World of Vegetarian Ramen Recipes

Ramen noodles are a comfort food for everyone in the world. It tends to be straightforward and economical, and you can make it extravagant and jam-loaded with beautiful and healthy vegetables and flavors. You should try all of these twenty yummy vegetarian recipes at home as they are easy to make and will surely make your day:

5.1 Japanese Spicy Vegetarian Ramen Recipe

Preparation Time: 30 minutes

Cooking Time: 10 minutes

Serving: 4

Ingredients:

- Chili paste, two tablespoon
- Sliced green onions, half cup
- Mirin paste, one teaspoon
- Fresh ginger, one teaspoon
- Miso paste, one tablespoon
- Chopped carrots, one cup
- Soy sauce, one tablespoon
- Shredded zucchini, one cup
- Blanched peas, one cup

- Chopped garlic, one teaspoon
- Japanese fresh herbs, half teaspoon
- Fresh shiso leaves, two tablespoon
- Fresh cilantro leaves, half cup
- Chopped tomatoes, half cup
- Ramen, as required

Instructions:

1. Add all the ingredients of the sauce i.e. miso paste, soy sauce, mirin paste and Japanese fresh herbs into a large pan.
2. Add the vegetables, chili paste, chopped tomatoes and the rest of the ingredients into the mixture.
3. Cook the dish for ten minutes.
4. Add the ramen into the mixture once the sauce is ready.
5. Mix the ramen well.
6. Cook the dish for five minutes.
7. Add the green onions into the dish.
8. Your dish is ready to be served.

5.2 Japanese Shiitake Mushroom Ramen Recipe

Preparation Time: 30 minutes

Cooking Time: 10 minutes

Serving: 4

Ingredients:

- Bean sprouts, one cup
- Sliced green onions, half cup
- Mirin paste, one teaspoon
- Cilantro, one cup
- Bamboo shoots, one teaspoon
- Miso paste, one tablespoon
- Shiitake mushrooms, one cup
- Soy sauce, one tablespoon
- Cooking oil, two tablespoon
- Chopped garlic, one teaspoon
- Japanese fresh herbs, half teaspoon
- Fresh shiso leaves, two tablespoon
- Fresh cilantro leaves, half cup
- Dried chili flakes, two teaspoon
- Soft boiled eggs, four
- Ramen, as required

Instructions:
1. Take a large pan.
2. Add the cooking oil and chopped garlic into the pan.
3. Add the shiitake mushrooms into the pan.

4. Add all the spices into the mixture.
5. Cook the ingredients for five minutes.
6. Add the bean sprouts and ramen into the mixture.
7. Cook all the ingredients well.
8. Peel the soft boiled eggs and add them into the mixture.
9. Cook for five minutes.
10. Garnish the dish with cilantro and green onions.
11. Your dish is ready to be served.

5.3 Japanese Miso Vegetarian Ramen Noodle Soup Recipe

Preparation Time: 20 minutes

Cooking Time: 20 minutes

Serving: 4

Ingredients:

- Ramen noodles, two packs
- Miso paste, one teaspoon
- Onion, one cup
- Bean sprouts, one cup
- Japanese fresh herbs, half teaspoon
- Water, one cup

- Minced garlic, two tablespoon
- Minced ginger, two tablespoon
- Cilantro, half cup
- Diced carrots, one cup
- Olive oil, two tablespoon
- Blanched peas, half cup
- Vegetable stock, two cups
- Chopped tomatoes, one cup

Instructions:
1. Take a pan.
2. Add in the oil and onions.
3. Cook the onions until they become soft and fragrant.
4. Add in the chopped garlic and ginger.
5. Cook the mixture and add the tomatoes into it.
6. Add the spices.
7. Add the miso paste into it when the tomatoes are done.
8. Mix the ingredients carefully and cover the pan.
9. Add the carrot, peas, bean sprouts and rest of the ingredients except the noodles.
10. Let the mixture boil.
11. Add the ramen noodles into the soup mixture.
12. Let the soup cook for ten to fifteen minutes straight.

13. Add cilantro on top.
14. Your dish is ready to be served.

5.4 Japanese Teriyaki Tofu Ramen Recipe

Preparation Time: 30 minutes
Cooking Time: 10 minutes
Serving: 4

Ingredients:

- Teriyaki sauce, one cup
- Sliced green onions, half cup
- Mirin paste, one teaspoon
- Cilantro, one cup
- Bamboo shoots, one teaspoon
- Miso paste, one tablespoon
- Soy sauce, one tablespoon
- Cooking oil, two tablespoon
- Chopped garlic, one teaspoon
- Japanese fresh herbs, half teaspoon
- Fresh shiso leaves, two tablespoon
- Fresh cilantro leaves, half cup
- Dried chili flakes, two teaspoon
- Tofu cubes, one cup

- Ramen, as required

Instructions:
1. Take a large pan.
2. Add the cooking oil and chopped garlic into the pan.
3. Add the tofu cubes into the pan.
4. Add all the spices into the mixture.
5. Cook the ingredients for five minutes.
6. Add the teriyaki sauce and ramen into the mixture.
7. Cook all the ingredients well.
8. Cover the pan for five minutes.
9. Garnish the dish with cilantro and green onions.
10. Your dish is ready to be served.

5.5 Japanese Tonkotsu Vegetarian Ramen Recipe

Preparation Time: 30 minutes

Cooking Time: 10 minutes

Serving: 4

Ingredients:

- Chopped chives, one teaspoon

- Butter, two tablespoon
- Tonkotsu broth, one cup
- Salt, to taste
- Black pepper, to taste
- Tamari paste, two teaspoon
- Mix vegetables, two cups
- Mirin paste, one tablespoon
- Chopped garlic, one teaspoon
- Ramen noodles, four packs

Instructions:
1. Take a large pan.
2. Add the butter and let it meltdown.
3. Add in the tamari paste.
4. Mix the tamari paste for two minutes.
5. Add the chopped garlic and mixed vegetables.
6. Add in the salt and pepper.
7. Add in the tonkotsu broth and rest of the ingredients in the end.
8. Mix all the ingredients well and then dish them out.
9. Garnish the fresh chopped chives on top.
10. Your dish is ready to be served.

5.6 Japanese Pantry Vegetarian Ramen Recipe

Preparation Time: 10 minutes
Cooking Time: 10 minutes
Serving: 4

Ingredients:

- Garlic powder, one teaspoon
- Soy sauce, a quarter cup
- Sliced green onions, half cup
- Ginger powder, one teaspoon
- Lemon juice, half cup
- Miso paste, one tablespoon
- Sirarcha sauce, two tablespoon
- Vegetables (of your choice), one cup
- Japanese fresh herbs, half teaspoon
- Ketchup, two tablespoon
- Fresh cilantro leaves, half cup
- Sliced scallions, half cup
- Ramen, as required
- Sesame oil, two tablespoon

Instructions:

1. Take a large saucepan.
2. Add the sesame oil and scallions into the pan.
3. Cook the scallions for a few minutes.
4. Add the garlic powder.
5. Add the ketchup and sirarcha into the mixture.
6. Cook the ingredients for two minutes.
7. Add the vegetables of your choice into the pan.
8. Cook the ingredients well.
9. Add the rest of the ingredients along with the ramen noodles.
10. Cook the mixture for ten minutes.
11. Garnish the ramen with green onions and cilantro on top.
12. Your dish is ready to be served.

5.7 Japanese Marinated Tofu and Vegetable Ramen Recipe

Preparation Time: 30 minutes

Cooking Time: 20 minutes

Serving: 4

Ingredients:

- Vegetable stock, two cups
- Crushed garlic, two
- Tofu cubes, one pound

- Salt, to taste
- Black pepper, to taste
- Olive oil, two tablespoon
- Dried white wine, one cup
- Onion, one cup
- All-purpose flour, three tablespoon
- Worcestershire sauce, two tablespoon
- Softened butter, three tablespoon
- Bay leaf, one
- Fresh thyme, two tablespoon
- Soy sauce, one cup
- Chopped cilantro, one cup
- Ramen noodles, four packs

Instructions:
1. Marinate the tofu cubes in soy sauce for ten to fifteen minutes.
2. Take a large skillet.
3. Add the oil and onions into the skillet.
4. Cook the onions until they turn golden brown.
5. Add the crushed garlic into the skillet.
6. Add the spices into the mixture.
7. Add all-purpose flour, Worcestershire sauce and dried white wine.
8. Add the butter and then add the vegetable stock and ramen noodles.

9. Add the tofu cubes into the ramen mixture.
10. Cook the mixture for ten minutes.
11. The dish is ready to be served.

5.8 Japanese Creamy Vegan Ramen Recipe

Preparation Time: 30 minutes
Cooking Time: 10 minutes
Serving: 4

Ingredients:

- Heavy cream, one cup
- Sliced green onions, half cup
- Mirin paste, one teaspoon
- Cilantro, one cup
- Fresh ginger, one teaspoon
- Miso paste, one tablespoon
- Soy sauce, one tablespoon
- Japanese fresh herbs, half teaspoon
- Chopped leeks, two tablespoon
- Tonkatsu broth, one cup
- Fresh cilantro leaves, half cup
- Minced lemon grass, one teaspoon
- Ramen, as required

Instructions:

1. Add all the ingredients of the sauce i.e. miso paste, soy sauce, mirin paste and Japanese fresh herbs into a large pan.
2. Add the heavy cream and the rest of the ingredients into the mixture.
3. Cook the dish for ten minutes.
4. Add the ramen into the mixture once the sauce is ready.
5. Mix the ramen well.
6. Close the lid of the instant pot.
7. Cook the dish for five more minutes.
8. Add the cilantro into the dish.
9. Your dish is ready to be served.

5.9 Japanese Creamy Sesame Ramen Broth Recipe

Preparation Time: 20 minutes

Cooking Time: 20 minutes

Serving: 4

Ingredients:

- Ramen noodles, two packs
- Miso paste, one teaspoon

- Onion, one cup
- Sesame seeds, one cup
- Japanese fresh herbs, half teaspoon
- Water, one cup
- Minced garlic, two tablespoon
- Minced ginger, two tablespoon
- Cilantro, half cup
- Heavy cream, one cup
- Olive oil, two tablespoon
- Water, half cup
- Vegetable stock, two cups
- Chopped tomatoes, one cup

Instructions:
1. Take a pan.
2. Add in the oil and onions.
3. Cook the onions until they become soft and fragrant.
4. Add in the chopped garlic and ginger.
5. Cook the mixture and add the tomatoes into it.
6. Add the spices.
7. Add the miso paste into it when the tomatoes are done.
8. Mix the ingredients carefully and cover the pan.
9. Add the sesame seeds and the rest of the ingredients except the noodles.

10. Let the mixture boil.
11. Add the ramen noodles and heavy cream into the broth mixture.
12. Let the broth cook for ten to fifteen minutes straight.
13. Add cilantro on top.
14. Your dish is ready to be served.

5.10 Japanese Spicy Broccoli Ramen Recipe

Preparation Time: 30 minutes
Cooking Time: 10 minutes
Serving: 4

Ingredients:

- Chili paste, two tablespoon
- Sliced green onions, half cup
- Mirin paste, one teaspoon
- Fresh ginger, one teaspoon
- Miso paste, one tablespoon
- Chopped broccoli, one cup
- Soy sauce, one tablespoon
- Chopped garlic, one teaspoon
- Japanese fresh herbs, half teaspoon
- Fresh shiso leaves, two tablespoon

- Fresh cilantro leaves, half cup
- Chopped tomatoes, half cup
- Ramen, as required

Instructions:
1. Add all the ingredients of the sauce i.e. miso paste, soy sauce, mirin paste and Japanese fresh herbs into a large pan.
2. Add the broccoli, chili paste, chopped tomatoes and the rest of the ingredients into the mixture.
3. Cook the dish for ten minutes.
4. Add the ramen into the mixture once the sauce is ready.
5. Mix the ramen well.
6. Cook the dish for five minutes.
7. Add the green onions into the dish.
8. Your dish is ready to be served.

5.11 Japanese Cauliflower Ramen Recipe

Preparation Time: 20 minutes
Cooking Time: 10 minutes
Serving: 4

Ingredients:

- Miso paste, half cup
- Sliced green onions, half cup
- Cauliflower florets, two cups
- Cilantro, one cup
- Fresh ginger, one teaspoon
- Soy sauce, one tablespoon
- Japanese fresh herbs, half teaspoon
- Fresh shiso leaves, two tablespoon
- Fresh cilantro leaves, half cup
- Minced lemon grass, one teaspoon
- Ramen, as required

Instructions:
1. Heat a large pan.
2. Add the cauliflower florets and the rest of the ingredients into the mixture.
3. Cook the ingredients for ten minutes.
4. Add the ramen into the mixture once the sauce is ready.
5. Mix the ramen well.
6. Cook the dish for five minutes.
7. Add the cilantro into the dish.
8. Your dish is ready to be served.

5.12 Japanese Hot and Sour Dashi Ramen Recipe

Preparation Time: 30 minutes
Cooking Time: 10 minutes
Serving: 4

Ingredients:

- Hot and sour sauce, one cup
- Sliced green onions, half cup
- Mirin paste, one teaspoon
- Fresh ginger, one teaspoon
- Miso paste, one tablespoon
- Dashi stock, one cup
- Soy sauce, one tablespoon
- Japanese fresh herbs, half teaspoon
- Fresh shiso leaves, two tablespoon
- Fresh cilantro leaves, half cup
- Chopped tomatoes, half cup
- Ramen, as required

Instructions:

1. Add all the ingredients of the sauce i.e. miso paste, soy sauce, mirin paste and Japanese fresh herbs into a large pan.

2. Add the dashi stock, hot and sour sauce, chopped tomatoes and the rest of the ingredients into the mixture.
3. Cook the dish for ten minutes.
4. Add the ramen into the mixture once the sauce is ready.
5. Mix the ramen well.
6. Cook the dish for five minutes.
7. Add the green onions into the dish.
8. Your dish is ready to be served.

5.13 Japanese Spicy Carrot Ramen Recipe

Preparation Time: 30 minutes
Cooking Time: 10 minutes
Serving: 4

Ingredients:

- Chili paste, two tablespoon
- Sliced green onions, half cup
- Mirin paste, one teaspoon
- Fresh ginger, one teaspoon
- Miso paste, one tablespoon
- Chopped carrots, one cup
- Soy sauce, one tablespoon
- Chopped garlic, one teaspoon

- Japanese fresh herbs, half teaspoon
- Fresh shiso leaves, two tablespoon
- Fresh cilantro leaves, half cup
- Chopped tomatoes, half cup
- Ramen, as required

Instructions:
1. Add all the ingredients of the sauce i.e. miso paste, soy sauce, mirin paste and Japanese fresh herbs into a large pan.
2. Add the carrots, chili paste, chopped tomatoes and the rest of the ingredients into the mixture.
3. Cook the dish for ten minutes.
4. Add the ramen into the mixture once the sauce is ready.
5. Mix the ramen well.
6. Cook the dish for five minutes.
7. Add the green onions into the dish.
8. Your dish is ready to be served.

5.14 Japanese Vegan Shōyu Ramen with Potatoes Recipe

Preparation Time: 20 minutes
Cooking Time: 20 minutes
Serving: 4

Ingredients:

- Ramen noodles, two packs
- Chopped potatoes, one cup
- Spicy chili bean sauce, two teaspoon
- Onion, one cup
- Dashi stock, two cups
- Japanese fresh herbs, half teaspoon
- Minced garlic, two tablespoon
- Minced ginger, two tablespoon
- Cilantro, half cup
- Chili oil, two tablespoon
- Shredded nori sheets, half cup
- Sheragi negi, two cups
- Chopped tomatoes, one cup

Instructions:
1. Take a pan.
2. Add in the oil and onions.
3. Cook the onions until they become soft and fragrant.
4. Add in the chopped garlic and ginger.
5. Cook the mixture for a few seconds.
6. Add the spices.
7. Add the sgeragi negi and chopped potatoes into it when the spices are done.
8. Mix the ingredients carefully and cover the pan.
9. Add the rest of the ingredients except the noodles.

10. Let the mixture boil.
11. Add the ramen noodles into the mixture.
12. Add shredded nori sheets on top.
13. Your dish is ready to be served.

5.15 Japanese Ginger Ramen Recipe

Preparation Time: 10 minutes

Cooking Time: 10 minutes

Serving: 4

Ingredients:

- Water, two cups
- Ramen noodles, two pack
- Ginger paste, one tablespoon
- Mix spice, half cup
- Dashi powder, two tablespoon
- Fresh shiso leaves, a quarter cup
- Sesame oil, one tablespoon

Instructions:
1. Take a large pan.
2. Add all the ingredients into the pan.
3. Cook the ingredients for ten minutes.
4. Garnish it with shiso leaves.
5. Your dish is ready to be served.

5.16 Japanese Vegan Ramen Taco Recipe

Preparation Time: 10 minutes

Cooking Time: 10 minutes

Serving: 4

Ingredients:

- Water, two cups
- Ramen noodle plates, two pack
- Mixed vegetables, one cup
- Ginger paste, one tablespoon
- Mix spice, half cup
- Dashi powder, two tablespoon
- Fresh shiso leaves, a quarter cup
- Sesame oil, one tablespoon

Instructions:
1. Take a large pan.
2. Add the vegetables and rest of the filling ingredients into the pan.
3. Cook the ingredients for ten minutes.
4. Switch off the stove.
5. Boil the ramen noodle plates in boiling water for one minute each.
6. Turn them into taco shape.
7. Add the prepared filling mixture into the taco.

8. Garnish the tacos with shiso leaves.
9. Your dish is ready to be served.

5.17 Japanese Vegetarian Spicy Peanut Tempeh Ramen Recipe

Preparation Time: 30 minutes
Cooking Time: 10 minutes
Serving: 4

Ingredients:

- Peanut sauce, one cup
- Sliced green onions, half cup
- Chili paste, one teaspoon
- Mirin paste, one teaspoon
- Cilantro, one cup
- Bamboo shoots, one teaspoon
- Miso paste, one tablespoon
- Soy sauce, one tablespoon
- Cooking oil, two tablespoon
- Chopped garlic, one teaspoon
- Japanese fresh herbs, half teaspoon
- Fresh shiso leaves, two tablespoon
- Fresh cilantro leaves, half cup
- Dried chili flakes, two teaspoon

- Tempeh cubes, one cup
- Ramen, as required

Instructions:

1. Take a large pan.
2. Add the cooking oil and chopped garlic into the pan.
3. Add the tempeh cubes into the pan.
4. Add all the spices into the mixture.
5. Cook the ingredients for five minutes.
6. Add the peanut sauce and ramen into the mixture.
7. Cook all the ingredients well.
8. Cover the pan for five minutes.
9. Garnish the dish with cilantro and green onions.
10. Your dish is ready to be served.

5.18 Japanese Spicy Soy Milk Ramen Recipe

Preparation Time: 30 minutes
Cooking Time: 10 minutes
Serving: 4

Ingredients:

- Soy milk, one cup

- Chili paste, one tablespoon
- Sliced green onions, half cup
- Mirin paste, one teaspoon
- Cilantro, one cup
- Fresh ginger, one teaspoon
- Miso paste, one tablespoon
- Soy sauce, one tablespoon
- Japanese fresh herbs, half teaspoon
- Fresh shiso leaves, two tablespoon
- Fresh cilantro leaves, half cup
- Minced lemon grass, one teaspoon
- Ramen, as required

Instructions:
1. Add all the ingredients of the sauce i.e. miso paste, soy sauce, mirin paste and Japanese fresh herbs into a large pan.
2. Add the soy milk and the rest of the ingredients into the mixture.
3. Cook the dish for ten minutes.
4. Add the ramen into the mixture once the sauce is ready.
5. Mix the ramen well.
6. Cook the dish for five minutes.
7. Add the cilantro into the dish.
8. Your dish is ready to be served.

5.19 Japanese Vegetarian Ginger and Scallion Ramen Recipe

Preparation Time: 10 minutes

Cooking Time: 10 minutes

Serving: 4

Ingredients:

- Water, two cups
- Ramen noodles, two pack
- Ginger slices, half cup
- Mix vegetables, one cup
- Chopped scallions, half cup
- Mix spice, half cup
- Dashi powder, two tablespoon
- Fresh shiso leaves, a quarter cup
- Sesame oil, one tablespoon

Instructions:

1. Take a large pan.
2. Add all the vegetables and oil into the pan.
3. Add the spices and sauces into the pan.
4. Cook the ingredients for five minutes and add the ramen noodles.
5. Cook the ingredients for ten minutes.

6. Garnish it with ginger slices and scallions on top.
7. Your dish is ready to be served.

5.20 Japanese Crispy Sesame Tofu Ramen Recipe

Preparation Time: 20 minutes
Cooking Time: 10 minutes
Serving: 4

Ingredients:

- Sesame seeds, half cup
- Sliced green onions, half cup
- Mirin paste, one teaspoon
- Cilantro, one cup
- Fresh ginger, one teaspoon
- Soy sauce, one tablespoon
- Japanese fresh herbs, half teaspoon
- Fresh shiso leaves, two tablespoon
- Fresh cilantro leaves, half cup
- Minced lemon grass, one teaspoon
- Ramen, as required
- Tofu cubes, one cup
- Corn starch, two teaspoon
- Cooking oil, as required

Instructions:
1. Heat a large pan.
2. Add the cooking oil and let it heat.
3. Mix the tofu cubes, sesame seeds and cornstarch in a bowl.
4. Add the tofu cubes into the heated oil.
5. Cook the tofu well for about five minutes.
6. Dish out the tofu cubes and set aside when done.
7. Add the miso paste and the rest of the ingredients into the mixture.
8. Cook the ingredients for ten minutes.
9. Add the ramen into the mixture once the sauce is ready.
10. Mix the ramen well.
11. Cook the dish for five minutes.
12. Add the crispy sesame tofu on top.
13. Add the cilantro into the dish.
14. Your dish is ready to be served.

Conclusion

Japanese noodle soups aka ramen is one of the easiest comfort food that you can prepare at home. Ramen soups come in different varieties. You can have vegetarian soups as well as non-vegetarian soups. All these soups are healthy and full of taste for ramen lovers around the world.

After reading this book, you will realize that making your favorite Japanese food at home is not difficult at all. In this book, we discussed in detail the history and origin of ramen. The various ingredients used in cooking ramen have also been mentioned in this book. This cookbook includes 70 recipes that contain breakfast, lunch, dinner, and vegetarian recipes. You can easily make these recipes at home without supervision of any kind. So, start cooking today and enjoy cooking your delicious ramen at home.

VIETNAMESE
COOKBOOK

70 Easy Recipes for Asian Foods from Vietnam.

Maki Blanc

© **Copyright 2021 by Maki Blanc - All rights reserved.**

This document is geared towards providing exact and reliable information in regard to the topic and issue covered. The publication is sold with the idea that the publisher is not required to render accounting, officially permitted, or otherwise, qualified services. If advice is necessary, legal or professional, a practiced individual in the profession should be ordered.

From a Declaration of Principles which was accepted and approved equally by a Committee of the American Bar Association and a Committee of Publishers and Associations.

In no way is it legal to reproduce, duplicate, or transmit any part of this document in either electronic means or in printed format. Recording of this publication is strictly prohibited and any storage of this document is not allowed unless with written permission from the publisher. All rights reserved.

The information provided herein is stated to be truthful and consistent, in that any liability, in terms of inattention or otherwise, by any usage or abuse of any policies, processes, or directions contained within is the solitary and utter responsibility of the recipient reader. Under no circumstances will any legal responsibility or blame be held against the publisher for any reparation, damages, or monetary loss due to the information herein, either directly or indirectly.

Respective authors own all copyrights not held by the publisher.

The information herein is offered for informational purposes solely and is universal as so. The presentation of the information is without contract or any type of guarantee assurance.

The trademarks that are used are without any consent, and the publication of the trademark is without permission or backing by the trademark owner. All trademarks and brands within this book are for clarifying purposes only and are owned by the owners themselves, not affiliated with this document.

Introduction

Although culinary art of Asian countries has long been globally admired for numerous delicious and elaborately-ornamented dishes, Vietnamese cuisine still wins the heart of numerous foodies nationally and internationally due to its fresh ingredients, refreshing taste and exquisite presentation.

Culinary culture is normally shaped by the way a society lives. The Vietnamese culture promotes the addition of various new flavors into their food. No explorers have yet succeeded in resisting the amazing flavors of Vietnamese dishes.

The food of the north is intensely inspired by China with its sautés and noodle-based soups. As you move to the south, there are more flavors of Thailand and Cambodia in the Vietnamese food. The heat and humidity in the south region of Vietnam is favorable for rice paddies, coconut forests, jackfruit trees, and spice gardens. The food in southern Vietnam is usually more flavorful i.e. better flavors for pho, more palm sugar utilized in exquisite dishes, and those well-known taffy-like coconut confectioners made with the help of coconut cream.

In this book, you will learn various different recipes originated from Vietnam. The recipe section will include breakfast, lunch, dinner, snacks, and sweet dishes. All these recipes are detailed with easy to follow instructions and detailed ingredients that help you out in cooking by these at home. So, start reading this amazing book now.

Chapter 1: The World of Vietnamese Breakfast Recipes

The morning meal in Vietnam is viewed as the main feast of the day. In various societies, they start the day with their own novel dishes. Following are the recipes listed below:

1.1 Vietnamese Fried Egg Recipe

Preparation Time: 30 minutes
Cooking Time: 10 minutes
Serving: 4

Ingredients:

- Spring onions, four
- Rice noodles, two cups
- Pepper to taste
- Butter, as required
- Salt to taste
- Baby plum tomatoes, four
- Eggs, four
- Cilantro, half cup

Instructions:
1. Boil the rice noodles according to the instructions on the package.
2. Once cooked, drain the noodles.
3. Put the butter in a pan.
4. Add the spring onions and chili into the small pan.
5. Cook for a couple of minutes until softened.

6. Whisk the milk and eggs in a bowl.
7. Add the eggs to the pan.
8. Fry the eggs.
9. Add the tomatoes and coriander leaves on top.
10. Once cooked, dish it out.
11. Add the eggs on top of the noodles.
12. The dish is ready to be served.

1.2 Vietnamese Breakfast Burgers Recipe

Preparation Time: 20 minutes
Cooking Time: 20 minutes
Serving: 4

Ingredients:

- Jalapenos, as required
- Chicken filet, four
- Mayonnaise, half cup
- Carrots, two
- Butter, two tablespoon
- Eggs, eight
- Burger buns, four
- Fish sauce, as required
- Cucumber, two
- Salt and pepper, to taste
- Cooking oil, as required

Instructions:
1. Take a large bowl.
2. Add the dry ingredients in a bowl.
3. Mix all the ingredients well.
4. Cook the chicken filet in a pan full of oil.

5. Dish out the chicken when it turns golden brown from both sides.
6. Toast the buns by adding a little butter on both sides.
7. Assemble the burgers.
8. Add all the ingredients one by one on top of the bun.
9. You can serve the burgers with any preferred sauce.
10. The dish is ready to be served.

1.3 Vietnamese Steamed Rice Rolls with Pork Recipe

Preparation Time: 30 minutes
Cooking Time: 15 minutes
Serving: 4

Ingredients:

- Thin soy sauce, one tablespoon
- Pepper powder, half tablespoon
- Sugar, one tablespoon
- Garlic powder, one tablespoon
- Fresh shallot, half tablespoon
- Milk, one cup
- Vegetable oil, one tablespoon
- Steamed rice, one cup
- Whole wheat flour, half cup
- Salt, to taste
- Water, to knead
- Pulled pork, one cup
- Yeast, two teaspoon

Instructions:

1. Take a bowl and add the steamed rice into it.
2. Then add the yeast and sugar into it.
3. Add lukewarm water in it.
4. Set aside for half hour.
5. Add the whole wheat flour into it.
6. Then add the salt and some water in it.
7. Then combine the ingredients to form a soft dough.
8. Meanwhile, mix the pulled pork and rest of the filling ingredients
9. Make round forms of dough with the help of the oil.
10. Add the mixture in middle of the dough and place on a tray.
11. Seam the rolls for fifteen minutes.
12. Your dish is ready to be served.

1.4 Vietnamese Crepes Recipe

Preparation Time: 10 minutes
Cooking Time: 15 minutes
Serving: 2

Ingredients:

- Almond milk, one cup
- Cilantro as required
- Almond oil, two tablespoon
- Tapioca flour, half cup
- Almond flour, half cup
- Eggs, three
- Arrowroot starch, half teaspoon

Instructions:

1. Mix in both the flours in a bowl.
2. Mix the ingredients carefully.
3. Add the mixture in small quantities in a pan.
4. Let the crepes turn golden on both sides.
5. Add a little cilantro on top of your crepes.
6. You can add fresh fruits as well on the top.
7. You can garnish the crepes with any other ingredient that you prefer.
8. Your dish is ready to be served.

1.5 Vietnamese Breakfast Bowl Recipe

Preparation Time: 10 minutes
Cooking Time: 20 minutes
Serving: 4

Ingredients:

- Coconut milk, half cup
- Wild blueberries, one cup
- Coconut oil, one tablespoon
- Sliced almonds, two tablespoon
- Milk, two cups
- Almond extract, one teaspoon
- Dry rolled oats, one cup
- Coconut cream, one cup

Instructions:
1. Combine all the ingredients together in a bowl.
2. Pour the mixture into a baking dish coated with coconut oil.
3. Add the one cup of frozen wild blueberries on top.
4. Sprinkle the sliced almonds on top.
5. Set the dishes on a flat sheet pan.

6. Bake for twenty-five minutes in a preheated oven.
7. When cooked, dish out and add fresh berries on top.
8. Your dish is ready to be served.

1.6 Vietnamese Happy Pancakes Recipe

Preparation Time: 20 minutes
Cooking Time: 20 minutes
Serving: 4

Ingredients:

- Sliced apples, one cup
- Sugar, four tablespoon
- Salt, as required
- Cilantro as required
- Sesame oil, two tablespoon
- Tapioca flour, half cup
- Almond flour, half cup
- Sliced peaches, one cup
- Coconut cream, a quarter cup
- Coconut milk, one cup

Instructions:
1. Mix in both the flours in a bowl.
2. Add the sliced peaches and apples into the bowl.
3. Add in the sugar and rest of the ingredients.
4. Mix the ingredients carefully.
5. Grease a pan with sesame oil.
6. Add the mixture in small quantities in a pan.
7. Let the pancakes turn golden on both sides.
8. Add a little cilantro on top of the pancakes.

9. You can garnish the pancakes with any other topping that you prefer.
10. Your dish is ready to be served.

1.7 Vietnamese Breakfast Pastries Recipe

Preparation Time: 2 hours
Cooking Time: 10 minutes
Serving: 4

Ingredients:

- Salt, to taste
- Pepper, to taste
- Milk, two cups
- White sugar, half cup
- Salt, one teaspoon
- Eggs, two
- Cooked ground pork, one cup
- Fish sauce, one teaspoon
- Oyster sauce, one teaspoon
- All-purpose flour, two cups
- Butter, one cup
- Dry yeast, one cup

Instructions:
1. Take a medium bowl and add the butter in it.
2. Add the flour and mix well.
3. Then refrigerate it.
4. Take a large bowl and add the yeast into it.

5. Add the sugar, salt and milk.
6. Mix the warm milk mixture with the flour and the yeast.
7. Add the eggs, the lemon extract and the almond extract together.
8. Then knead it in the flour until the dough is formed.
9. Place butter on dough and fold it.
10. Make pastries from the dough roll.
11. Take a small bowl.
12. Add the pork, salt, pepper and the sauces.
13. Add the pork mixture in the pastry dough.
14. Bake them for ten minutes.
15. The pastry is ready to be served.

1.8 Vietnamese Scrambled Eggs with Fish Sauce Recipe

Preparation Time: 30 minutes
Cooking Time: 10 minutes
Serving: 4

Ingredients:

- Onions, one
- Chopped garlic, one teaspoon
- Butter, two tablespoon
- Fish sauce, half cup
- Mixed vegetables, half pound
- Salt, to taste
- Black pepper, to taste
- Chopped fresh chives, as required
- Eggs, twelve

Instructions:
1. Take a large pan.
2. Add the butter and let it meltdown.
3. Add in the chopped onion.
4. Cook the onion until soft.
5. Add in the garlic.
6. Mix the onions and garlic for two minutes and add in the mixed vegetables.
7. Add the eggs and let them cook.
8. Scramble the mixture.
9. Add in the salt and pepper.
10. Add in the fish sauce in the end.
11. When the eggs are done, dish them out.
12. Add the fresh chopped chives on top.
13. Your dish is ready to be served.

1.9 Vietnamese Steak and Eggs Recipe

Preparation Time: 10 minutes
Cooking Time: 20 minutes
Serving: 4

Ingredients:

- Powdered garlic, half teaspoon
- Eggs, four
- Steak meat, half pound
- Turmeric, half teaspoon
- Mixed vegetables, one cup
- Sea salt, to taste
- Coconut oil, two tablespoon
- Mixed spice, half teaspoon
- Onion, one
- Fish sauce, one tablespoon

- Oyster sauce, two tablespoon
- Dried thyme, half teaspoon
- Powdered ginger, half teaspoon

Instructions:
1. Heat the coconut oil in a pan.
2. Add the steak meat.
3. Dish out the meat when done and slice it up.
4. Add the mixed vegetables and spices.
5. Once they turn soft, add in the eggs as well.
6. Add the spices and cook it for five to ten minutes or until the eggs are cooked.
7. Add in the sliced steaks.
8. Mix the dish well and cook for five minutes.
9. Your dish is ready to be served.

1.10 Vietnamese Scrambled Eggs with Pork Mince Recipe

Preparation Time: 30 minutes
Cooking Time: 10 minutes
Serving: 4

Ingredients:

- Onions, one
- Chopped garlic, one teaspoon

- Butter, two tablespoon
- Fish sauce, half cup
- Oyster sauce, half tablespoon
- Mixed spices, one tablespoon
- Pork mince, half pound
- Salt, to taste
- Black pepper, to taste
- Chopped fresh chives, as required
- Eggs, twelve

Instructions:
1. Take a large pan.
2. Add the butter and let it meltdown.
3. Add in the chopped onion.
4. Cook the onion until soft.
5. Add in the garlic.
6. Mix the onions and garlic for two minutes and add in the minced pork.
7. Add the eggs and let it cook.
8. Scramble the mixture.
9. Add in the salt, mixed spice and pepper.
10. Add in the fish sauce and the oyster sauce in the end.
11. When the eggs are done dish them out.
12. Add the fresh chopped chives on top.
13. Your dish is ready to be served.

1.11 Vietnamese Breakfast Egg Rolls Recipe

Preparation Time: 15 minutes
Cooking Time: 25 minutes
Serving: 4

Ingredients:

- Cooked eggs, three
- Canola oil, one cup
- Minced garlic, two tablespoon
- Chopped red onion, one cup
- Coconut milk, one cup
- Lime juice, two tablespoon
- Water, as required
- Wonton wrappers, as required
- Cilantro leaves, as required
- Salt, a pinch

Instructions:
1. Take a bowl.
2. Add the eggs and garlic powder.
3. Add more oil into it and add all the ingredients.
4. Add the chopped red onions, coconut milk and water as required.
5. Add the lime juice and cilantro leaves into it.
6. Add the salt and pepper as required.
7. Add the ingredients into the wrappers and roll them.
8. Serve the rolls with soy sauce.
9. Your dish is ready to be served.

1.12 Vietnamese Tofu Pancakes Recipe

Preparation Time: 20 minutes
Cooking Time: 20 minutes
Serving: 4

Ingredients:

- Ground garlic, half teaspoon
- Salt, as required
- Black pepper, two
- Ground pepper, as required
- Red onion, one
- Cilantro as required
- Sesame oil, two tablespoon
- Tapioca flour, half cup
- Almond flour, half cup
- Shredded tofu, one cup
- Coconut milk, one cup
- Fish sauce, half teaspoon
- Ground ginger, half teaspoon

Instructions:
15. Mix in both the flours in a bowl.
16. Add the chopped red onions.
17. Add the shredded tofu into the bowl.
18. Add in the spices, black pepper, fish sauce and cilantro.
19. Mix the ingredients carefully.
20. Grease a pan with sesame oil.
21. Add the mixture in small quantities in a pan.
22. Let the pancakes turn golden on both sides.
23. Add a little cilantro on top of your pancakes.
24. Your dish is ready to be served.

Chapter 2: The World of Vietnamese Lunch Recipes

Large numbers of the most famous Vietnamese dishes can be made very easily at home. Following are some classic Vietnamese recipes that are rich in healthy nutrients and you can easily make them with the detailed instructions list in each recipe:

2.1 Vietnamese Prawn and Papaya Salad Recipe

Preparation Time: 10 minutes
Cooking Time: 30 minutes
Serving: 2

Ingredients:

- Prawn pieces, half pound
- Maple syrup, one teaspoon
- Ground ginger, a quarter teaspoon
- Papaya, two
- Mixed nuts, two tablespoon
- Pepper, as required
- Cilantro, half cup
- Salt, a quarter teaspoon
- Soy sauce, as required
- Mint leaves, half cup
- Salad dressing, half cup

Instructions:
1. Peel the papaya and then cut into large pieces.

2. Boil the prawn pieces, drain them and slice them into a bowl.
3. Mix all the ingredients along with the prawns and papaya.
4. In a bowl, add the salad dressing and beat it well.
5. Drizzle the dressing on top of the prawns and papaya mixture.
6. Your dish is ready to be served.

2.2 Vietnamese Chicken Salad Recipes

Preparation Time: 10 minutes
Cooking Time: 30 minutes
Serving: 2

Ingredients:

- Chicken pieces, half pound
- Maple syrup, one teaspoon
- Ground ginger, a quarter teaspoon
- Mixed fruit, half cup
- Mixed nuts, two tablespoon
- Pepper, as required
- Cilantro, half cup
- Salt, a quarter teaspoon
- Soy sauce, as required
- Mint leaves, half cup
- Salad dressing, half cup

Instructions:
1. Peel the fruits and then cut them into large pieces.
2. Boil the chicken pieces, drain them and slice them into a bowl.
3. Mix all the ingredients along with the chicken and fruits.
4. In a bowl, add the salad dressing and beat it well.
5. Drizzle the dressing on top of the chicken and fruit mixture.
6. Your dish is ready to be served.

2.3 Vietnamese Herb Salad Recipe

Preparation Time: 10 minutes
Cooking Time: 30 minutes
Serving: 2

Ingredients:

- Parsley leaves, half pound
- Maple syrup, one teaspoon
- Sliced celery, a quarter teaspoon
- Fresh dill leaves, half cup
- Roasted cashews, half cup
- Pepper, as required
- Cilantro, half cup
- Salt, a quarter teaspoon
- Soy sauce, as required
- Basil leaves, half cup
- Fresh fruit as required
- Salad dressing, half cup

Instructions:
1. Peel the leaves and then cut them into large pieces.
2. Mix all the ingredients along with the leaves and fruits.
3. In a bowl, add the salad dressing and beat it well.
4. Drizzle the dressing on top of the leaves and fruit mixture.
5. Your dish is ready to be served.

2.4 Vietnamese Summer Rolls with Peanut Dipping Sauce Recipe

Preparation Time: 10 minutes
Cooking Time: 20 minutes
Serving: 2

Ingredients:

- Olive oil, two cups
- Garlic powder, one tablespoon
- Salt to taste
- Pepper to taste
- Paprika, one tablespoon
- Onion diced, one cup
- Parsley, one tablespoon
- Pork meat, one cup
- Tomatoes, one cup
- Jalapeno slices, as required
- Peanut dipping sauce, one cup
- Avocado slices, as required
- Tortilla sheets, four

Instructions:
1. Add the olive oil into a pan.
2. Heat the oil well.
3. Add the onions.
4. Cook the onions well until they turn soft.
5. Add parsley, garlic powder, paprika and tomatoes.
6. Cook them for five minutes.
7. Cook the mixture again and keep stirring.
8. Add pieces of pork meat.
9. Continue to cook the ingredients for few minutes.
10. Lay the mixture onto a tortilla sheet.
11. Add the peanut dipping sauce on top of the meat.
12. Add the rest of the ingredients on top and roll it into a roll.
13. Heat the roll.
14. You can serve it with any other sauce of your choice.
15. Your dish is ready to be served.

2.5 Vietnamese Pork Meatballs Recipe

Preparation Time: 30 minutes
Cooking Time: 10 minutes
Serving: 4

Ingredients:

- Soy sauce, two tablespoon
- Eggs, two
- Salt, to taste
- Black pepper, to taste
- Milk, one cup
- Onion, one cup

- Bread crumbs, one cup
- Sugar, two tablespoon
- Minced pork meat, one pound
- Minced ginger, two tablespoon
- Cayenne pepper, a dash
- Butter, two tablespoon
- All-purpose flour, five tablespoon

Instructions:
1. Take a large bowl.
2. Add the oil and onions into the bowl.
3. Add the chopped ginger into the bowl.
4. Add the minced pork into the bowl.
5. Add the spices, eggs and bread crumbs.
6. Mix all the ingredients together.
7. Shape the pork mixture into round meatballs.
8. Heat a grilling pan.
9. Add the olive oil on top.
10. Place the meatballs on top.
11. Fry the meatballs on both sides until it turns golden brown.
12. Fry all the meatballs and dish them out.
13. The dish is ready to be served.

2.6 Vietnamese Chicken Pho Recipe

Preparation Time: 30 minutes
Cooking Time: 20 minutes
Serving: 4

Ingredients:

- Shredded chicken, one cup
- Onion, one cup

- Rice noodles, one cup
- Chinese paprika, half teaspoon
- Water, one cup
- Minced garlic, two tablespoon
- Minced ginger, two tablespoon
- Cilantro, half cup
- Olive oil, two tablespoon
- Water, half cup
- Chicken stock, half cup
- Chopped tomatoes, one cup

Instructions:
1. Take a pan.
2. Add in the oil and onions.
3. Cook the onions until they become soft and fragrant.
4. Add in the chopped garlic and ginger.
5. Cook the mixture and add the tomatoes into it.
6. Add the spices.
7. When the tomatoes are done, add the shredded chicken and stock into it.
8. Mix the ingredients carefully and cover your pan.
9. Add the rice noodles into the mixture.
10. Add the water into the mixture and cover the pan.
11. Let the pho cook for ten to fifteen minutes straight.
12. Add cilantro on top.
13. Your dish is ready to be served.

2.7 Vietnamese Baked Snapper Recipe

Preparation Time: 10 minutes

Cooking Time: 25 minutes
Serving: 2

Ingredients:

- Powdered cumin, one tablespoon
- Salt, to taste
- Black pepper, to taste
- Turmeric powder, one teaspoon
- Onion, one cup
- Smoked paprika, half teaspoon
- Hoison sauce, half cup
- Snapper pieces, one pound
- Minced garlic, two tablespoon
- Minced ginger, two tablespoon
- Cilantro, half cup
- Olive oil, two tablespoon
- Oyster sauce, three tablespoon
- Roasted peanuts, half cup

Instructions:
1. Take a large bowl.
2. Add the oil and onions into the bowl.
3. Add the chopped garlic and ginger into the bowl.
4. Add the tomatoes into the bowl.
5. Add the spices.
6. Add the cilantro into it.
7. Mix all the ingredients together.
8. Cover your snapper pieces with the mixture above.
9. Bake your snapper pieces.
10. Dish them out when cooked properly.
11. Sprinkle some cilantro and roasted peanuts on top.

12. You can serve it with any of your preferred sauces.
13. Your dish is ready to be served.

2.8 Vietnamese Stir-Fried Sweet Shrimp Recipe

Preparation Time: 30 minutes
Cooking Time: 10 minutes
Serving: 4

Ingredients:

- Fish broth, one cup
- Honey, one teaspoon
- Onion, one cup
- Brown sugar, two tablespoon
- Smoked paprika, half teaspoon
- Water, one cup
- Shrimps, two cups
- Mixed spices, two tablespoon
- Minced garlic, two tablespoon
- Minced ginger, two tablespoon
- Cilantro, half cup
- Olive oil, two tablespoon
- Chopped tomatoes, one cup

Instructions:
1. Take a pan.
2. Add in the oil and onions.
3. Cook the onions until they become soft and fragrant.
4. Add in the chopped garlic and ginger.
5. Cook the mixture and add the tomatoes into it.

6. Add the spices, honey, sugar and sauces.
7. When the tomatoes are done, add the shrimps into it.
8. Cook for five minutes.
9. When cooked, dish it out.
10. Garnish your dish with chopped cilantro leaves
11. Your dish is ready to be served.

2.9 Vietnamese Lemongrass and Tamarind Chicken Recipe

Preparation Time: 30 minutes
Cooking Time: 10 minutes
Serving: 4

Ingredients:

- Cilantro, half cup
- Sesame oil, two tablespoon
- Chopped tomatoes, one cup
- Lemon juice, one cup
- Powdered cumin, one tablespoon
- Salt, to taste
- Black pepper, to taste
- Lemongrass, one teaspoon
- Onion, one cup
- Vegetable broth, one cup
- Chinese paprika, half teaspoon
- Chicken cubes, two cup
- Tamarind paste, half cup
- Minced garlic, two tablespoon
- Minced ginger, two tablespoon

Instructions:
1. Take a pan.
2. Add in the oil and onions.
3. Cook the onions until they become soft and fragrant.
4. Add in the chopped garlic and ginger.
5. Cook the mixture and add the tomatoes into it.
6. Add the spices.
7. When the tomatoes are done, add the chicken cubes into it.
8. Cook for five minutes.
9. Add in the lemongrass and tamarind paste.
10. Add in the broth and lemon juice.
11. Mix the ingredients carefully and cover the pan.
12. When cooked, dish it out.
13. Garnish the dish with chopped cilantro leaves
14. Your dish is ready to be served.

2.10 Vietnamese Marinated Lamb Chops Recipe

Preparation Time: 10 minutes
Cooking Time: 25 minutes
Serving: 2

Ingredients:

- Lemon juice, one tablespoon
- Salt, to taste

- Black pepper, to taste
- Mix spice, one teaspoon
- Onion, one cup
- Smoked paprika, half teaspoon
- Lamb chops, one pound
- Minced garlic, two tablespoon
- Minced ginger, two tablespoon
- Cilantro, half cup
- Olive oil, two tablespoon

Instructions:
1. Take a large bowl.
2. Add the oil and onions into the bowl.
3. Add the chopped garlic and ginger into the bowl.
4. Add the spices.
5. Add the cilantro into it.
6. Mix all the ingredients together.
7. Add the lamb chops into the mixture.
8. Cook the lamb chops.
9. Dish them out when cooked properly.
10. Sprinkle some cilantro on top.
11. Your dish is ready to be served.

2.11 Vietnamese Cabbage Soup Recipe

Preparation Time: 30 minutes
Cooking Time: 20 minutes
Serving: 4

Ingredients:

- Sliced cabbage, one cup
- Eggs, two
- Onion, one cup

- Chinese paprika, half teaspoon
- Water, one cup
- Minced garlic, two tablespoon
- Minced ginger, two tablespoon
- Cilantro, half cup
- Olive oil, two tablespoon
- Water, half cup
- Vegetable stock, half cup
- Chopped tomatoes, one cup

Instructions:
1. Take a pan.
2. Add in the oil and onions.
3. Cook the onions until they become soft and fragrant.
4. Add in the chopped garlic and ginger.
5. Cook the mixture and add the tomatoes into it.
6. Add the spices.
7. When the tomatoes are done, add the sliced cabbage and stock into it.
8. Mix the ingredients carefully and cover your pan.
9. Let the soup cook for ten to fifteen minutes straight.
10. Add cilantro on top.
11. Your dish is ready to be served.

2.12 Vietnamese Mixed Vegetables Recipe

Preparation Time: 30 minutes
Cooking Time: 10 minutes
Serving: 4

Ingredients:

- Chopped tomatoes, one cup
- Cauliflower, one cup
- Mix spice powder, one teaspoon
- Onion, one cup
- Fish sauce, a quarter cup
- Oyster sauce, a quarter cup
- Brussel sprouts, one cup
- Smoked paprika, half teaspoon
- Chopped carrots, one cup
- Minced garlic, two tablespoon
- Minced ginger, two tablespoon
- Lemon juice, half cup
- Chopped bell peppers, one cup
- Olive oil, two tablespoon

Instructions:
1. Take a pan.
2. Add in the oil and onions.
3. Cook the onions until they become soft and fragrant.
4. Add in the chopped garlic and ginger.
5. Cook the mixture and add the tomatoes to it.
6. Add the spices.
7. When the tomatoes are done, add the vegetables into it.
8. Mix the ingredients carefully and cover the pan.
9. When your vegetables are done, dish them out.
10. Add cilantro on top.
11. Your dish is ready to be served.

2.13 Vietnamese Fried Rice Recipe

Preparation Time: 10 minutes
Cooking Time: 25 minutes
Serving: 2

Ingredients:

- Minced garlic, two tablespoon
- Minced ginger, two tablespoon
- Cilantro, half cup
- Cooked rice, one cup
- Olive oil, two tablespoon
- Coconut cream, three tablespoon
- Chopped tomatoes, one cup
- Water, one cup
- Fish sauce, one teaspoon
- Onion, one cup
- Coconut milk, one cup
- Smoked paprika, half teaspoon
- Water, one cup

Instructions:
1. Take a pan.
2. Add in the oil and onions.
3. Cook the onions until they become soft and fragrant.
4. Add in the chopped garlic and ginger.
5. Cook the mixture and add the tomatoes into it.
6. Add the spices.
7. When the tomatoes are done, add the coconut milk into it.
8. Add in the water.
9. Mix the ingredients carefully and cover your pan.
10. Add in the rice and into the mixture.

11. Fry the rice and let it cook for an additional five minutes.
12. Add cilantro on top.
13. Your dish is ready to be served.

2.14 Vietnamese Pork Chops Recipe

Preparation Time: 10 minutes
Cooking Time: 20 minutes
Serving: 2

Ingredients:

- Fish sauce, half teaspoon
- Water, half cup
- Pork chops, one pound
- Minced garlic, two tablespoon
- Minced ginger, two tablespoon
- Cilantro, half cup
- Olive oil, two tablespoon
- Chopped tomatoes, one cup
- Lemon juice, one cup
- Oyster sauce, one tablespoon
- Salt, to taste
- Black pepper, to taste
- Mix spice, one teaspoon
- Onion, one cup
- pork broth, one cup

Instructions:
1. Take a pan.
2. Add in the oil and onions.
3. Cook the onions until they become soft and fragrant.

4. Add in the chopped garlic and ginger.
5. Cook the mixture and add the tomatoes into it.
6. Add the spices.
7. When the tomatoes are done, add the pork chops into it.
8. Add in the water and lemon juice.
9. Mix the ingredients carefully and cover the pan.
10. Garnish the dish with chopped cilantro.
11. Your dish is ready to be served.

2.15 Vietnamese Instant Pho Soup Recipe

Preparation Time: 30 minutes
Cooking Time: 20 minutes
Serving: 4

Ingredients:

- Pork, two cup
- Onion, one cup
- Rice noodles, one cup
- Oyster sauce, half teaspoon
- Water, one cup
- Minced garlic, two tablespoon
- Minced ginger, two tablespoon
- Cilantro, half cup
- Fish sauce, two tablespoon
- Olive oil, two tablespoon
- Chicken stock, half cup
- Chopped tomatoes, one cup

Instructions:
1. Take an instant pot.
2. Add in the oil and onions.

3. Cook the onions until they become soft and fragrant.
4. Add in the chopped garlic and ginger.
5. Cook the mixture and add the tomatoes into it.
6. Add the spices.
7. When the tomatoes are done, add the minced pork and stock into it.
8. Mix the ingredients carefully and cover your pot.
9. Let the pho cook for ten to fifteen minutes straight.
10. Add the rice noodles into the pot and cook for five minutes.
11. Add cilantro on top.
12. Your dish is ready to be served.

Chapter 3: The World of Vietnamese Dinner Recipes

Vegetables and noodles are the standard eating routine in many families in the cities of Vietnam. A typical Vietnamese feast will usually incorporate rice, a meat or fish dish, soups and vegetables. Following are some classic dinner recipes that are rich in healthy nutrients and you can easily make them with the detailed instructions list in each recipe:

3.1 Vietnamese Sambal Kangkung with Shrimp Paste Recipe

Preparation Time: 30 minutes
Cooking Time: 10 minutes
Serving: 4

Ingredients:

- Sambal olek, one tablespoon
- Cilantro, half cup
- Sesame oil, two tablespoon
- Chopped tomatoes, one cup
- shrimp paste, one cup
- Powdered cumin, one tablespoon
- Salt, to taste
- Black pepper, to taste
- Lemongrass, one teaspoon
- Chinese paprika, half teaspoon
- Diced kangkung, one pound
- Tamarind paste, half cup
- Minced garlic, two tablespoon
- Minced ginger, two tablespoon

Instructions:
1. Take a pan.
2. Add in the oil and onions.
3. Cook the onions until they become soft and fragrant.
4. Add in the chopped garlic and ginger.
5. Cook the mixture and add the tomatoes into it.
6. Add the spices.
7. When the tomatoes are done, add the kangkung and shrimp paste into it.
8. Cook for five minutes.
9. Add in the sambal olek, lemongrass and tamarind paste.
10. Mix the ingredients carefully and cover the pan.
11. When cooked, dish it out.
12. Garnish the dish with chopped cilantro leaves
13. Your dish is ready to be served.

3.2 Vietnamese Pomelo and Shrimp Salad Recipe

Preparation Time: 10 minutes
Cooking Time: 30 minutes
Serving: 2

Ingredients:

- Cooked shrimps, half pound
- Bean sprouts, one cup
- Sliced celery, a quarter teaspoon
- Fresh basil leaves, half cup

- Pomelo pulp, half cup
- Pepper, as required
- Cilantro, half cup
- Salt, a quarter teaspoon
- Soy sauce, as required
- Bird's eye chili, half cup
- Salad dressing, half cup

Instructions:
1. Cut the bean sprouts into large pieces.
2. Mix all the ingredients along with the shrimps.
3. In a bowl, add the salad dressing and beat it well.
4. Drizzle the dressing on top of the shrimps.
5. Your dish is ready to be served.

3.3 Vietnamese Pork Bone and Green Papaya Soup Recipe

Preparation Time: 10 minutes
Cooking Time: 10 minutes
Serving: 4

Ingredients:

- Chopped white onions, one cup
- Chopped green papaya, one pound
- Chicken stock, one quart
- Unsalted butter, three tablespoon
- Pork bones, half pound
- Fresh cilantro, as required
- Fresh herbs, half cup
- Dried thyme, one teaspoon
- Minced garlic, one teaspoon
- Fish sauce, half teaspoon

- Oyster sauce, two tablespoon

Instructions:
1. Take a large pan.
2. Add the chopped onions in the butter.
3. When soft and translucent, add in the minced garlic.
4. Add in the stock, and rest of the ingredients.
5. Add in all the rest of the ingredients and cook the ingredients until the papaya is cooked.
6. Remove the bone pieces.
7. Blend the soup well.
8. Cook the soup for an extra few minutes.
9. Add the soup in a serving bowl.
10. You can also garnish it with chopped fresh cilantro.
11. The dish is ready to be served.

3.4 Vietnamese Beef and Noodle Salad Recipe

Preparation Time: 10 minutes
Cooking Time: 25 minutes
Serving: 4

Ingredients:

- Cooked beef cubes, one cup
- Carrot sliced, one cup
- Red bell pepper sliced, one cup
- Ginger, one tablespoon
- Garlic powder, two teaspoon
- Fish sauce, half teaspoon
- Sesame oil, one teaspoon
- Soy sauce, one teaspoon

- Sriracha, one tablespoon
- Lime juice, one tablespoon
- Rice noodles, one pack
- Salt, to taste
- Pepper, to taste

Instructions:
1. Take a large bowl and add beef cubes into it.
2. Add the ginger and garlic powder.
3. Mix well.
4. Add the carrot slices and red bell pepper into it.
5. Add the salt and pepper as you like.
6. Add the sesame oil and mix well so that a homogeneous mixture is obtained.
7. Add the sriracha and rest of the ingredients into the mixture.
8. Mix all the ingredients.
9. Your salad is ready to be served.

3.5 Vietnamese Lamb Shanks with Sweet Potatoes Recipe

Preparation Time: 30 minutes
Cooking Time: 10 minutes
Serving: 4

Ingredients:

- Cooked sweet potatoes, two cup
- Mix spice, one teaspoon
- Onion, one cup
- Smoked paprika, half teaspoon
- Chinese dried chilies, half cup
- Minced garlic, two tablespoon
- Minced ginger, two tablespoon

- Lemon juice, half cup
- Oyster sauce, half cup
- Lamb shanks, half pound
- Olive oil, two tablespoon
- Chopped tomatoes, one cup

Instructions:
1. Take a pan.
2. Add in the oil and onions.
3. Cook the onions until they become soft and fragrant.
4. Add in the chopped garlic and ginger.
5. Cook the mixture and add the tomatoes into it.
6. Add the spices.
7. When the tomatoes are done, add the sweet potato and rest of the ingredients into it.
8. Mix the ingredients carefully.
9. Add cilantro on top.
10. Your dish is ready to be served.

3.6 Vietnamese Spiced Duck Salad Recipe

Preparation Time: 10 minutes
Cooking Time: 10 minutes
Serving: 2

Ingredients:

- Roasted duck, half pound
- Spicy red sauce, one cup
- Sliced celery, a quarter teaspoon
- Fresh basil leaves, half cup
- Sirarcha, half cup
- Pepper, as required
- Cilantro, half cup
- Salt, a quarter teaspoon
- Soy sauce, as required
- Bird's eye chili, half cup
- Salad dressing, half cup

Instructions:
1. Cut the duck meat into large pieces.
2. Mix all the ingredients along with the duck meat.
3. In a bowl, add the salad dressing and beat it well.
4. Drizzle the dressing on top of the meat.
5. Your dish is ready to be served.

3.7 Vietnamese Seafood Salad Recipe

Preparation Time: 10 minutes
Cooking Time: 10 minutes
Serving: 2

Ingredients:

- Mixed seafood, half pound
- Wine vinegar, one cup
- Caster sugar, a quarter teaspoon
- Spring onions, half cup
- Bean sprouts, two cups
- Sirarcha, half cup
- Pepper, as required
- Cilantro, half cup
- Salt, a quarter teaspoon
- Soy sauce, as required
- Bird's eye chili, half cup
- Salad dressing, half cup

Instructions:
1. Cook your seafood by boiling it well.
2. Mix all the ingredients along with the bean sprouts and spring onions.
3. In a bowl, add the salad dressing and beat it well.
4. Drizzle the dressing on top of the mixture.
5. Your dish is ready to be served.

3.8 Vietnamese Caramel Trout Recipe

Preparation Time: 30 minutes
Cooking Time: 10 minutes
Serving: 4

Ingredients:

- Brown sugar, one tablespoon
- Cilantro, half cup
- Sesame oil, two tablespoon
- Chopped tomatoes, one cup
- Rainbow trout, one cup
- Oyster sauce, one tablespoon
- Salt, to taste
- Black pepper, to taste
- Lemongrass, one teaspoon
- Chinese paprika, half teaspoon
- Steamed rice, one cup
- Minced garlic, two tablespoon
- Minced ginger, two tablespoon

Instructions:
1. Take a pan.
2. Add in the oil and onions.
3. Cook the onions until they become soft and fragrant.
4. Add in the chopped garlic and ginger.
5. Cook the mixture and add the tomatoes into it.
6. Add the spices.
7. When the tomatoes are done, add the trout into it.
8. Cook for five minutes.
9. Add in the brown sugar, lemongrass and steamed rice.
10. Mix the ingredients carefully and cover the pan.
11. When cooked, dish it out.

12. Garnish the dish with chopped cilantro leaves.
13. Your dish is ready to be served.

3.9 Vietnamese Veggie Hotpot Recipe

Preparation Time: 20 minutes
Cooking Time: 20 minutes
Serving: 4

Ingredients:

- Oyster sauce, one tablespoon
- Chinese chili peppers, two
- Fish sauce, one tablespoon
- Soy sauce, half tablespoon
- Minced garlic, two teaspoon
- Cooking oil, three tablespoon
- Hot sauce, half cup
- Mixed vegetables, two cups
- Salt, as required
- Chopped fresh cilantro, as required

Instructions:
1. Take a large pan.
2. Add the cooking oil into the pan and heat it.
3. Add the vegetables into the pan and stir-fry it.
4. Add the minced garlic along with the vegetables.
5. Add the soy sauce, fish sauce, Chinese chili peppers, hot sauce and rest of the ingredients into the mixture.
6. Cook your dish for ten minutes.
7. Dish out your vegetables and garnish them with chopped fresh cilantro leaves.

8. Your dish is ready to be served.

3.10 Vietnamese Prawn and Noodle Salad with Crispy Shallots Recipe

Preparation Time: 10 minutes
Cooking Time: 25 minutes
Serving: 4

Ingredients:

- Cooked prawns, one cup
- Carrot sliced, one cup
- Red bell pepper sliced, one cup
- Ginger, one tablespoon
- Garlic powder, two teaspoon
- Fish sauce, half teaspoon
- Sesame oil, one teaspoon
- Soy sauce, one teaspoon
- Sriracha, one tablespoon
- Lime juice, one tablespoon
- Rice noodles, one pack
- Salt, to taste
- Pepper, to taste
- Shallots, half cup

Instructions:
1. Take a large bowl and add prawns into it.
2. Add the ginger and garlic powder.
3. Mix well.
4. Add the carrot slices and red bell pepper into it.
5. Add the salt and pepper as you like.
6. Add the sesame oil and mix well so that a homogeneous mixture is obtained.

7. Add the sriracha and rest of the ingredients into the mixture.
8. Fry the shallots in oil until they turn crispy.
9. Add the shallots on top of the mixture.
10. Your salad is ready to be served.

3.11 Vietnamese Lemongrass Chicken Recipe

Preparation Time: 30 minutes
Cooking Time: 10 minutes
Serving: 4

Ingredients:

- Cilantro, half cup
- Sesame oil, two tablespoon
- Chopped tomatoes, one cup
- Lemon juice, one cup
- Fish sauce, one tablespoon
- Salt, to taste
- Black pepper, to taste
- Lemongrass, one teaspoon
- Onion, one cup
- Vegetable broth, one cup
- Chinese paprika, half teaspoon
- Chicken cubes, two cup
- Minced garlic, two tablespoon
- Minced ginger, two tablespoon

Instructions:
1. Take a pan.
2. Add in the oil and onions.
3. Cook the onions until they become soft and fragrant.

4. Add in the chopped garlic and ginger.
5. Cook the mixture and add the tomatoes into it.
6. Add the spices.
7. When the tomatoes are done, add the chicken cubes into it.
8. Cook for five minutes.
9. Add in the lemongrass.
10. Add in the broth and lemon juice.
11. Mix the ingredients carefully and cover the pan.
12. When cooked, dish it out.
13. Garnish the dish with chopped cilantro leaves
14. Your dish is ready to be served.

3.12 Vietnamese Garlic Butter Noodles Recipe

Preparation Time: 30 minutes
Cooking Time: 10 minutes
Serving: 4

Ingredients:

- Butter, one tablespoon
- Cilantro, one cup
- Fresh ginger, one teaspoon
- Fish sauce, one tablespoon
- Soy sauce, one tablespoon
- Oyster sauce, half teaspoon
- Chili garlic sauce, two tablespoon
- Fresh cilantro leaves, half cup
- Fresh basil leaves, a quarter cup
- Vegetable broth, one cup

- Rice noodles, as required

Instructions:
1. Add all the ingredients of the sauce into a wok.
2. Cook your ingredients.
3. Add the noodles into the mixture once the sauce is ready.
4. Mix the noodles well and cook it for five minutes.
5. Add the cilantro into the dish.
6. Your dish is ready to be served.

3.13 Vietnamese Papaya Salad Recipe

Preparation Time: 10 minutes
Cooking Time: 30 minutes
Serving: 2

Ingredients:

- Maple syrup, one teaspoon
- Ground ginger, a quarter teaspoon
- Papaya, two
- Mixed nuts, two tablespoon
- Pepper, as required
- Cilantro, half cup
- Salt, a quarter teaspoon
- Soy sauce, as required
- Mint leaves, half cup
- Salad dressing, half cup

Instructions:

7. Peel the papaya and then cut into large pieces.
8. Mix all the ingredients along with the papaya.
9. In a bowl, add the salad dressing and beat it well.
10. Drizzle the dressing on top of the papaya mixture.
11. Your dish is ready to be served.

3.14 Vietnamese Purple Yam Soup Recipe

Preparation Time: 10 minutes
Cooking Time: 30 minutes
Serving: 4

Ingredients:

- Chopped white onions, one cup
- Purple yam, one pound
- Fresh chopped cilantro, half cup
- Unsalted butter, three tablespoon
- Oyster sauce, one teaspoon
- Minced garlic, one teaspoon
- Fish sauce, half teaspoon
- Coconut milk, half cup
- Coconut cream, one cup

Instructions:
1. In a large pan, add the chopped onions in the butter.
2. Add in the minced garlic when onions are soft and translucent.
3. Add in the purple yam.
4. Add in all the rest of the ingredients and cook the ingredients until the purple yams are cooked.
5. Blend the soup well.

6. Cook for an extra few minutes.
7. The dish is ready to be served.

3.15 Vietnamese Fried Tofu Recipe

Preparation Time: 30 minutes
Cooking Time: 10 minutes
Serving: 4

Ingredients:

- Cilantro, half cup
- Olive oil, two tablespoon
- Chopped tomatoes, one cup
- Lemon juice, half cup
- Mix spice powder, one tablespoon
- Salt, to taste
- Black pepper, to taste
- Fish sauce, one teaspoon
- Onion, one cup
- Tofu cubes, one cup
- Oyster sauce, half teaspoon
- Minced garlic, two tablespoon

Instructions:
1. Take a pan.
2. Add in the oil and onions.
3. Cook the onions until they become soft and fragrant.
4. Add in the chopped garlic.
5. Cook the mixture and add the tomatoes into it.
6. Add the spices and sauces.
7. When the tomatoes are done, add the tofu cubes into it.
8. Cook for five minutes.

9. When cooked, dish it out.
10. Garnish your dish with chopped cilantro leaves.
11. Your dish is ready to be served.

3.16 Vietnamese Noodle Soup Recipe

Preparation Time: 10 minutes
Cooking Time: 20 minutes
Serving: 4

Ingredients:

- Minced garlic, two tablespoon
- Minced ginger, two tablespoon
- Cilantro, half cup
- Diced carrots, one cup
- Olive oil, two tablespoon
- Beef broth, half cup
- Fish sauce, half cup
- Vegetable stock, half cup
- Chopped tomatoes, one cup
- Chicken broth, one cup
- Hot sauce, half cup
- Onion, one cup
- Bell peppers, one cup
- Noodles, half pound
- Oyster sauce, half teaspoon
- Soy sauce, one cup

Instructions:
1. Take a pan.
2. Add in the oil and onions.

3. Cook the onions until they become soft and fragrant.
4. Add in the chopped garlic and ginger.
5. Cook the mixture and add the tomatoes into it.
6. Add the sauces.
7. When the tomatoes are done, add the noodles into it.
8. Add in both chicken and beef broth.
9. Mix the ingredients carefully and cover your pan.
10. Add the vegetables into the mixture.
11. Add the water into the mixture and cover the pan.
12. Let the soup cook for ten to fifteen minutes straight.
13. Add the cilantro on top.
14. Your dish is ready to be served.

3.17 Vietnamese Shaking Beef Recipe

Preparation Time: 30 minutes
Cooking Time: 20 minutes
Serving: 4

Ingredients:

- Sesame oil, two tablespoon
- Sugar, one teaspoon
- Oyster sauce, two tablespoon
- Pepper to taste
- Salt, as required
- Chinese cooking wine, two teaspoon
- Soy sauce, two tablespoon
- Beef, two pounds
- Vegetable oil, two tablespoon

- Cornstarch, two tablespoon

Instructions:
1. Add the oil in a large pan.
2. Add in the beef and cook it properly.
3. Add the rest of the ingredients.
4. In the end add the cornstarch and once the dish thickens, switch off the heat.
5. Your dish is ready to be served.

3.18 Vietnamese Tomato and Pineapple Fish Soup Recipe

Preparation Time: 30 minutes
Cooking Time: 20 minutes
Serving: 4

Ingredients:

- Diced pineapple, one cup
- Deboned fish, two cups
- Onion, one cup
- Oyster sauce, half teaspoon
- Water, one cup
- Minced garlic, two tablespoon
- Soy sauce, two tablespoon
- Cilantro, half cup
- Olive oil, two tablespoon
- Water, half cup
- Vegetable stock, half cup
- Cherry tomatoes, one cup

Instructions:
1. Take a pan.
2. Add in the oil and onions.
3. Cook the onions until they become soft and fragrant.
4. Add in the chopped garlic.
5. Cook the mixture and add the cherry tomatoes into it.
6. Add the spices and sauces.
7. When the tomatoes are done, add the diced pineapple and fish into it.
8. Mix in the rest of the ingredients and cover your pan.
9. Let the soup cook for ten to fifteen minutes straight.
10. Add cilantro on top.
11. Your dish is ready to be served.

Chapter 4: The World of Vietnamese Dessert Recipes

If you are a dessert lover and want to enjoy new flavors and tastes, you are in for a treat with various Vietnamese sweets. Ordinarily low in sugar and made with solid ingredients, you will track down a wide collection of sweet alternatives in the Vietnamese cuisine. Following are some yummy dessert recipes that are rich in healthy nutrients:

4.1 Vietnamese Pandan Rice and Mung Bean Cake Recipe

Preparation Time: 10 minutes
Cooking Time: 20 minutes
Serving: 4

Ingredients:

- Sweet pandan rice, two cup
- Salt, a pinch
- Bread flour, half cup
- Coconut milk, one cup
- Lime zest, as required
- Pepper, to taste
- Mung bean paste, one cup
- Baking powder, one teaspoon
- Vanilla essence, half teaspoon
- Soy sauce, one tablespoon

Instructions:
1. Add the bread flour into a large bowl.

2. Cook the pandan rice in the rice cooking pan.
3. Add the rice into the bowl when it is cooked. Then mix them.
4. Add the lime zest as required.
5. Add the cilantro if required.
6. Add some water and boil the whole mixture for ten minutes.
7. Cool the mixture and then add the vanilla essence, baking powder and coconut milk into it.
8. Mix the ingredients.
9. Add the batter into the cupcake molds.
10. Add the mung bean paste in the center of the mixture.
11. Bake the rice cake.
12. Dish out the cake when it is done.
13. Your dish is ready to be served.

4.2 Vietnamese Peanut Sticky Rice Recipe

Preparation Time: 20 minutes
Cooking Time: 20 minutes
Serving: 4

Ingredients:

- Cooked rice, one bowl
- Cilantro, as required
- Baking powder, four teaspoon
- Coconut flakes, one and a half cup
- Baking soda, one teaspoon
- Buttermilk, two cups
- Peanut essence, two drops
- Roasted peanuts, one cup

- White sugar, one cup
- Water, two cups
- Tapioca flour, one cup
- Coconut cream, half cup

Instructions:
1. Add the tapioca flour into a large bowl.
2. Add the white sugar into the mixture as required.
3. Add the baking powder and beat the mixture for five more minutes.
4. Add the water in a separate bowl.
5. Add coconut flakes into it.
6. Add the coconut cream into the mixture.
7. Add the cooked rice into it.
8. Mix them thoroughly until a homogeneous mixture is obtained.
9. Add the peanut essence and roasted peanuts.
10. Mix the rice well.
11. Your dish is ready to be served.

4.3 Vietnamese Mung Bean Dumplings Recipe

Preparation Time: 50 minutes
Cooking Time: 30 minutes
Serving: 4

Ingredients:

- Mung bean paste, two cups
- Thin soy sauce, one tablespoon
- Cinnamon powder, half tablespoon
- Sweet vinegar, one tablespoon

- Milk, one cup
- Vegetable oil, one tablespoon
- All-purpose flour, one cup
- Whole wheat flour, half cup
- Salt, to taste
- Water, to knead

Instructions:
1. Take a bowl and add the flour into it.
2. Add lukewarm water in it.
3. Set aside for half an hour.
4. Take the whole wheat flour.
5. Then add the salt and milk in it.
6. Then combine the ingredients to form a soft dough.
7. Knead it for ten minutes.
8. Take a small bowl.
9. Add the thin soy sauce, cinnamon powder, sweet vinegar and mung bean paste in the bowl.
10. Make round forms of dough with the help of the oil.
11. Add the mung bean mixture in between.
12. Steam your dumplings for ten minutes.
13. Once the dumplings are steamed, take them out.
14. Your dish is ready to be served.

4.4 Vietnamese Pandan Waffles Recipe

Preparation Time: 30 minutes
Cooking Time: 10 minutes
Serving: 4

Ingredients:

- Rice flour, one cup
- Eggs, two
- Chopped fresh cilantro, half cup
- Coconut milk, one cup
- Salt to taste
- Pandan leaves, half cup
- Pandan essence, two tablespoon

Instructions:
1. Heat your waffle maker.
2. Beat the egg yolks in a separate bowl.
3. Add in the egg yolks in the egg whites and delicately mix them with a spatula.
4. Combine the eggs and the rest of the ingredients.
5. When your waffle maker is heated adequately, pour in the mixture.
6. Close your waffle maker.
7. Let your waffle cook for five to six minutes approximately.
8. When your waffles are done, dish them out.
9. Add the chopped cilantro leaves on top of the waffles.
10. Your dish is ready to be served.

4.5 Vietnamese Three Color Dessert Recipe

Preparation Time: 10 minutes
Cooking Time: 20 minutes

Serving: 4

Ingredients:

- Green color, three drops
- Red color, three drops
- Yellow color, three drops
- Rice, one cup
- Baking powder, four teaspoon
- Coconut milk, one cup
- All-purpose flour, one and a half cup
- Baking soda, one teaspoon
- Eggs, two
- Brown sugar, one cup
- Tapioca starch, one tablespoon
- Salt, to taste

Instructions:
1. Add the eggs in a large bowl.
2. Beat the eggs until they turn frothy.
3. Add the baking powder and coconut milk into it.
4. Add the brown sugar and beat the mixture for five more minutes.
5. In a separate bowl, add all the dried ingredients.
6. Mix them thoroughly.
7. Cook your mixture until it turns thick.
8. Cook the rice in rice cooking pan.
9. Divide the rice in three portions and add the colors.
10. Add the rice into the formed mixture.
11. Your dish is ready to be served.
12.

4.6 Vietnamese Fruit Cocktail Recipe

Preparation Time: 10 minutes
Cooking Time: 20 minutes
Serving: 4

Ingredients:

- Strawberries, half cup
- Banana slices, one cup
- Plain yogurt, half cup
- Milk, half cup
- Apples, half cup
- Melon, half cup
- Mixed fruit juice, half cup
- Ice cubes, as required

Instructions:
1. Take a blender and add the milk into it.
2. Add the banana slices into it.
3. Blend it for few minutes.
4. Then add the plain yogurt into it.
5. Add the fruit juice into it.
6. In the end, add the strawberries, melon and apples into it.
7. Your dish is ready to be served.

4.7 Vietnamese Sweet Corn Pudding Recipe

Preparation Time: 10 minutes
Cooking Time: 20 minutes
Serving: 4

Ingredients:

- Sweet corn, one cup
- Baking powder, four teaspoon
- Barley flakes, one and a half cup
- Baking soda, one teaspoon
- Buttermilk, two cups
- White sugar, one cup
- Water, two cups
- Tapioca flour, one cup
- Coconut cream, half cup

Instructions:
1. Add the tapioca flour into a large bowl.
2. Add the sweet corns into the mixture.
3. Add the white sugar and beat the mixture for five more minutes.
4. In a separate bowl, add all the dried ingredients.
5. Add the water into it
6. Add the coconut cream into the mixture.
7. Mix them thoroughly until a consistent mixture is formed.
8. Check the thickness of pudding and add extra sugar if required.
9. Your dish is ready to be served.

4.8 Vietnamese Banana Tapioca Recipe

Preparation Time: 10 minutes
Cooking Time: 20 minutes
Serving: 4

Ingredients:

- Sliced bananas, one cup
- Rice, one cup
- Baking powder, four teaspoon
- Coconut milk, one cup
- All-purpose flour, one and a half cup
- Baking soda, one teaspoon
- Eggs, two
- Brown sugar, one cup
- Tapioca starch, one tablespoon
- Salt, to taste

Instructions:
1. Add the eggs in a large bowl.
2. Beat the eggs until they turn frothy.
3. Add the baking powder and coconut milk into it.
4. Add the brown sugar and beat the mixture for five more minutes.
5. Add all the dried ingredients in a separate bowl.
6. Mix both the dried and wet ingredients thoroughly.
7. Cook the mixture.
8. Add the rice into the mixture and cook.
9. Put the banana slices on cooked rice.
10. Your dish is ready to be served.

4.9 Vietnamese Sesame Balls Recipe

Preparation Time: 10 minutes
Cooking Time: 40 minutes
Serving: 4

Ingredients:

- Salted butter, one cup
- Black sesame seeds, one cup
- Yeast, one tablespoon
- Large eggs, two
- Kosher salt, half teaspoon
- Almond slices, one cup
- Vanilla extract, one teaspoon
- Flour, three and a half cup
- White sugar, half cup

Instructions:
1. Take a large bowl and put the black sesame seeds into it.
2. Add the dry ingredients in the bowl.
3. Mix all the ingredients well.
4. Add the white sugar and yeast in a bowl with two tablespoon of hot water.
5. Place the yeast mixture in a damp place.
6. Add the butter into the wet ingredients.
7. Add the yeast mixture, sliced almonds and eggs into the cookie mixture.
8. Add the formed mixture into a pipping bag.
9. Make small round balls on a baking dish and bake the balls.
10. Your dish is ready to be served.

4.10 Vietnamese Sponge Cake Recipe

Preparation Time: 30 minutes
Cooking Time: 25 minutes
Serving: 4

Ingredients:

- Vanilla sauce, one cup
- Butter, half cup
- Sugar, a quarter cup
- Ground cardamom, a quarter teaspoon
- Flour, one cup
- Baking soda, a pinch
- Egg, one

Instructions:
1. Make the cake batter by mixing all the ingredients in a large bowl.
2. Make the batter and pour it into a baking dish.
3. Make sure the baking dish is properly greased and lined with parchment papers.
4. Bake the cake.
5. When cooked, dish it out.
6. Cut the cake into slices.
7. The dish is ready to be served.

4.11 Vietnamese Milkshake Recipe

Preparation Time: 10 minutes
Cooking Time: 20 minutes
Serving: 4

Ingredients:

- Avocado cubes, half cup
- Banana slices, one cup
- Plain yogurt, half cup
- Milk, half cup
- Coconut milk, half cup
- Ice cubes, as required

Instructions:
1. Take a blender and add the milk into it.
2. Add the banana slices into it.
3. Blend it for few minutes.
4. Then add the plain yogurt into it.
5. Add the coconut milk into it.
6. In the end, add the avocado cubes into it.
7. Blend the milkshake well.
8. Your dish is ready to be served.

4.12 Vietnamese Ice Cream Recipe

Preparation Time: 10 minutes
Cooking Time: 20 minutes
Serving: 4

Ingredients:

- Coffee paste, half cup
- Whole milk, half cup
- Cocoa powder, two tablespoon
- Rock sugar, half cup
- Vanilla extract, one teaspoon

Instructions:
1. Take a bowl and add the milk into it.
2. Add the sugar as required.
3. Mix them thoroughly.
4. Heat the mixture, and add the coffee paste into it.
5. Refrigerate your mixture for one night.
6. Put the cocoa powder on it.
7. Your dish is ready to be served.

4.13 Vietnamese Taro Pudding Recipe

Preparation Time: 10 minutes
Cooking Time: 20 minutes
Serving: 4

Ingredients:

- Taro roots, one cup
- Baking powder, four teaspoon
- Barley flakes, one and a half cup
- Baking soda, one teaspoon
- Buttermilk, two cups
- White sugar, one cup
- Water, two cups
- Tapioca flour, one cup
- Coconut cream, half cup

Instructions:
1. Add the tapioca flour into a large bowl.
2. Add the taro roots into the mixture.

3. Add the white sugar and beat the mixture for five more minutes.
4. In a separate bowl, add all the dried ingredients.
5. Add the water into it
6. Add the coconut cream into the mixture.
7. Mix them thoroughly until a homogeneous mixture is obtained.
8. Check the thickness of pudding and add extra sugar if required.
9. Your dish is ready to be served.

4.14 Vietnamese Sticky Rice Recipe

Preparation Time: 20 minutes
Cooking Time: 20 minutes
Serving: 4

Ingredients:

- Cooked rice, one bowl
- Cilantro, as required
- Baking soda, four teaspoon
- Coconut flakes, one and a half cup
- Baking soda, one teaspoon
- Buttermilk, two cups
- White sugar, one cup

- Water, two cups
- Tapioca flour, one cup
- Coconut cream, half cup

Instructions:
1. Add the tapioca flour into a large bowl.
2. Add the white sugar into the mixture as required.
3. Add the baking soda and beat the mixture for five more minutes.
4. In a separate bowl, add the water in it.
5. Add coconut flakes into it.
6. Add the coconut cream into the mixture.
7. Add the cooked rice into it.
8. Mix them thoroughly until a homogeneous mixture is obtained.
9. Mix the rice well.
10. Your dish is ready to be served.

4.15 Vietnamese Donuts Recipe

Preparation Time: 50 minutes
Cooking Time: 40 minutes
Serving: 2

Ingredients:

- Eggs, two
- Yeast, half cup
- Sesame powder, one tablespoon
- Maple syrup, one tablespoon
- Coconut milk, half cup
- White sugar, half cup

- Salt, one teaspoon
- Vanilla extract, one tablespoon
- Cake flour, two cups
- Butter, one cup

Instructions:
1. Take a medium bowl and add the eggs, sesame powder and the cake flour in it.
2. Add the one cup coconut milk and mix well.
3. Add the sugar, the salt and the beaten eggs.
4. Mix them well.
5. Mix the warm milk mixture with the flour and the coconut.
6. Add the eggs and vanilla extract together.
7. Add the yeast into the whole mixture.
8. When dough is formed, roll it in your desired shape.
9. Place the donuts on a greased baking tray.
10. Bake the donuts for twenty minutes.
11. Your dish is ready to be served.

Chapter 5: The World of Vietnamese Snack Recipes

Vietnamese snacks have a deep rooted place in the culture of Vietnam. Following are some amazing Vietnamese snack recipes that are rich in healthy nutrients and you can easily make them with the detailed instructions list in each recipe:

5.1 Crispy Vietnamese Fish Cakes Recipe

Preparation Time: 30 minutes
Cooking Time: 25 minutes
Serving: 4

Ingredients:

- All-purpose flour, one cup
- Crab meat, one cup
- Baking powder, one tablespoon
- Baking soda, half tablespoon
- Egg, two
- Milk, one cup
- Bread crumbs, one cup
- Vegetable oil, one cup
- Salt, half tablespoon
- Oil, one cup

Instructions:
1. Take a large bowl and add the all-purpose flour in it
2. Add the crab meat in it and mix well.
3. Add the baking powder, and salt into it.
4. Mix well until a good mixture is obtained.

5. Take another bowl and add the eggs into it.
6. Add the milk and a little oil into it.
7. Combine them well so that good mixture is formed.
8. Form round balls from the crab mixture and then dip them into the egg mixture.
9. Coat them with the bread crumbs.
10. Fry the balls until a light brown color comes.
11. Serve the cakes with your preferred sauce or dip.
12. Your dish is ready to be served.

5.2 Crispy Vietnamese Lettuce Cups Recipe

Preparation Time: 20 minutes
Cooking Time: 10 minutes
Serving: 4

Ingredients:

- Chopped coriander, a quarter cup
- Mint leaves, half cup
- Lettuce leaves, as required
- Cooked beef, one cup
- Lemongrass, one tablespoon
- Garlic powder, one tablespoon
- Milk, one cup
- Vegetable oil, one tablespoon
- Lemon juice, half cup
- Fish sauce, half cup
- Fried shallots, one tablespoon
- Salt, to taste
- Black pepper, as required
- Brown sugar, one tablespoon

- Cucumber, one cup
- Cooked noodles, one cup

Instructions:
1. Take a large bowl.
2. Add all the ingredients together into the bowl except the lettuce wraps.
3. Mix all the ingredients well to form a mixture.
4. Add the mixture into the lettuce wraps.
5. Fold the lettuce wraps.
6. Serve your wraps with soy sauce or any other sauce or dip you prefer.
7. Your dish is ready to be served.

5.3 Vietnamese Beef and Mango Salad Recipe

Preparation Time: 10 minutes
Cooking Time: 20 minutes
Serving: 4

Ingredients:

- Vietnamese salad dressing, two cups
- Minced ginger, two tablespoon
- Lemon juice, half cup
- Cilantro, one cup
- Olive oil, two tablespoon
- Chopped tomatoes, one cup
- Beef chunks, one cup
- Turmeric powder, one teaspoon
- Onion, one cup
- Mango cubes, one cup
- Soy sauce, half teaspoon

- Chopped avocado, one cup
- Minced garlic, two tablespoon

Instructions:
1. Peel and cut the mango into cubes.
2. Take a pan.
3. Add in the oil and onions.
4. Cook the onions until they become soft and fragrant.
5. Add in the chopped garlic and ginger.
6. Cook the mixture and add the tomatoes into it.
7. Add the spices.
8. When the tomatoes are done, add the beef chunks into it.
9. Mix the ingredients carefully.
10. When your beef is done, dish them out.
11. Peel and cut the avocado.
12. Place the chopped avocado and beef in a bowl.
13. Mix all the ingredients together.
14. Add the Vietnamese salad dressing on top of the salad.
15. Garnish your salad with the chopped cilantro.
16. Your dish is ready to be served.

5.4 Vietnamese Prawn and Lime Mayo Wrap Recipe

Preparation Time: 30 minutes
Cooking Time: 10 minutes
Serving: 4

Ingredients:

- Olive oil, half cup
- Chopped parsley, half cup
- Fish sauce, half cup
- Grated ginger, two tablespoon
- Lemon juice, two tablespoon
- Cabbage leaves, as required
- Cooked and shredded prawn meat, one cup
- Chopped orange, one
- Shredded carrots, one cup
- Green onion, one cup
- Chopped bell peppers, a quarter cup
- Orange juice, half cup
- Tortilla wraps, as required
- Lime mayo sauce, as required
- Balsamic vinegar, half cup

Instructions:
1. Add the balsamic vinegar, orange juice, chopped parsley, rosemary stalks, grated ginger, fish sauce and lemon juice in a large bowl.
2. Mix the ingredients together and keep it aside.
3. In the next bowl, add in the rest of the ingredients and mix well.
4. Add the sauce formed above.
5. Mix your filling and sauce.
6. Add the salad mixture onto your tortilla wraps and roll it.

7. Heat the wrap and drizzle extra sauce on top of the wrap.
8. Your dish is ready to be served.

5.5 Vietnamese Rice Paper Rolls Recipe

Preparation Time: 30 minutes
Cooking Time: 50 minutes
Serving: 4

Ingredients:

- Ginger, one tablespoon
- Rice paper, as required
- Quinoa, half cup
- Chai egg, one
- Fish sauce, one tablespoon
- Avocado slices, two
- Carrot slices, one cup
- Beetroot, one
- Radish, one cup
- Garlic powder, two teaspoon
- Maple syrup, half teaspoon
- Sesame oil, one teaspoon
- Salt, to taste
- Pepper, to taste

Instructions:

1. Take a large bowl and add the radishes and carrots slices into it.

2. Add the ginger and garlic powder.
3. Mix well until a good mixture is obtained.
4. Add the chai egg and quinoa into it and mix gently.
5. Add the lime juice, maple syrup and Japanese red chili.
6. Add the salt and pepper as you prefer.
7. Add the sesame oil, red bell peppers and mix well.
8. Add the pepper into the mixture for taste.
9. Add the avocado slices in the end and put the mixture on rice paper.
10. Make rolls by folding the rice papers.
11. Your dish is ready to be served.

5.6 Vietnamese Pickled Bitter Melon Salad Recipe

Preparation Time: 10 minutes
Cooking Time: 30 minutes
Serving: 2

Ingredients:

- Maple syrup, one teaspoon
- Ground ginger, a quarter teaspoon
- Picked bitter melon, two cups
- Mixed nuts, two tablespoon
- Pepper, as required
- Cilantro, half cup
- Salt, a quarter teaspoon
- Soy sauce, as required
- Mint leaves, half cup
- Salad dressing, half cup

Instructions:
1. Cut the pickled melon into large pieces.
2. Mix all the ingredients along with the melon.
3. Add the salad dressing in a bowl and beat it well.
4. Drizzle the dressing on top of the melon mixture.
5. Your dish is ready to be served.

5.7 Vietnamese Spring Rolls Recipe

Preparation Time: 40 minutes
Cooking Time: 10 minutes
Serving: 2

Ingredients:

- Rice vermicelli, one pound
- Rice wrappers, five
- Shrimp, half pound
- Fresh Thai basil, half teaspoon
- Water, one cup
- Lime juice, one tablespoon
- White sugar, two tablespoon
- Hoisin Sauce, two teaspoon
- Chopped peanuts, one tablespoon
- Garlic chili sauce, half tablespoon
- Minced garlic, one teaspoon
- Oil, for frying

Instructions:
1. Take a saucepan and add the water in it.
2. Boil the water then add the rice vermicelli.
3. Boil it and drain it after five minutes.
4. Take boiling water in large bowl.

5. Dip the wrapper into it.
6. Lay the wrapper flat and add the shrimp on top of the wrapper.
7. Add the rice vermicelli, basil and mint on top.
8. Add the lettuce and cilantro on it.
9. Roll the wrapper tightly and make sure that there is no hole in the roll.
10. Deep fry the rolls.
11. Dish out the rolls when they turn golden brown.
12. Mix the water, hoisin sauce, peanuts, garlic, lime juice and sugar to make a sauce.
13. Drizzle the sauce on top of the spring rolls or serve it along the rolls.
14. Your dish is ready to be served.

5.8 Vietnamese Chicken Baguettes Recipe

Preparation Time: 10 minutes
Cooking Time: 30 minutes
Serving: 6

Ingredients:

- Chicken, one pound
- Olive oil, one teaspoon
- Rice vinegar, one teaspoon
- Golden sugar, half tablespoon
- Spring onions, two
- Carrot, half
- Lime juice, one tablespoon
- Cucumber, two
- Baguette bread, as required
- Sweet chili sauce, one tablespoon

- Gem lettuce leaves, three
- Red chili, half teaspoon

Instructions:
1. Take a pan and add the olive oil in it.
2. Heat it and cook the chicken in it for two minutes.
3. Mix the rice vinegar and sugar and lime juice in the pan.
4. Add more sugar if needed.
5. Add the carrot, spring onions and cucumber in it.
6. Add chili per taste.
7. Split the sandwich baguette completely.
8. Stuff it with the gem leaves.
9. Add the chicken mixture on top.
10. Cover the chicken with the bread slice and toast your sandwich.
11. Serve the dish with chili sauce.

5.9 Vietnamese Fish Sauce Recipe

Preparation Time: 5 minutes
Cooking Time: 10 minutes
Serving: 4

Ingredients:

- Water, five tablespoon

- Sugar two tablespoon
- Minced garlic, one teaspoon
- Lemon juice, two tablespoon
- Fish sauce, two tablespoon

Instructions:
1. Take a bowl and add the water in it.
2. Add the sugar into it and dissolve it well.
3. Heat the water on low heat.
4. Add the lemon juice as required.
5. Then in the end, add the fish sauce.
6. Top it with the garlic and chilies.
7. Your dish is ready to be served.

5.10 Vietnamese Shrimp Tacos Recipe

Preparation Time: 30 minutes
Cooking Time: 30 minutes
Serving: 4

Ingredients:

For slaw:
- Sour cream, half cup
- Mayonnaise, a quarter cup
- Lime juice, a quarter teaspoon

- Flour, one cup
- Red onion, one cup
- Chopped cilantro, one tablespoon
- Flour tortillas, five
- Tomato salsa, half cup
- Broccoli, half cup

For the filling:
- Sugar, half cup
- Canola oil, half cup
- Shrimp, one pound
- Lime zest, a pinch
- Cumin, half teaspoon
- Chili Powder, one tablespoon
- Garlic powder, one teaspoon
- Onion powder, one teaspoon
- Dried oregano, half teaspoon
- Salt, half teaspoon

Instructions:
1. Take a large bowl and add the canola oil into it.
2. Add the sugar and salt as required.
3. Add the garlic powder and onion powder into it.
4. Add the cumin and lime zest in the same bowl
5. Mix them all thoroughly.
6. Then coat the shrimp into it and refrigerate it for thirty minutes.
7. Make slaw in a bowl by adding mayonnaise and sour cream.
8. Add the broccoli, chili and cilantro into it.
9. Mix well and season with salt.
10. Cover it and refrigerate.

11. Wrap the tortillas in foil and bake for ten minutes.
12. Cook the shrimps for three to five minutes.
13. Divide the shrimps among tortillas, top with slaw.
14. Your dish is ready to be served.

Conclusion

With a solid Chinese impact in large numbers of the dishes, the Vietnamese food is fragrant and brimming with flavor. In the last few years, Vietnamese food has gotten increasingly more well-known throughout the world. Foodies may have attempted the two most popular Vietnamese dishes: spring rolls and bread rolls. Rice, noodles, vegetables and spices all have a huge part in Vietnamese food, making it one of the best cooking in the world.

In Vietnam, you will find one undeniable truth which is that the Vietnamese love eating noodles a lot. They eat them consistently, sometimes for each supper. Vietnamese noodles are produced using a couple of fundamental ingredients, the most well-known being rice, wheat and mung beans.

Vietnamese food is not only quite unlike any other food in Southeast Asia but also regarded as one of the healthiest cuisines all over the world. Tasting Vietnamese delicious foods, tourists have chance to enjoy its uniqueness through five senses: food arrangement appealing to eyes, sounds coming from crisp ingredients, five spices lingering on the tongue, aromatic ingredients from herbs attracting the nose and some food merely being perceived by touching.

This book covers the variety of Vietnamese dishes, making it easy for the readers to prepare their favourite recipes in their kitchen without any stress. This cookbook incorporates 70 healthy plans that contain Vietnamese breakfast recipes, Vietnamese lunch and dinner recipes, Vietnamese snack recipes and Vietnamese dessert recipes that you can undoubtedly make at home very easily. So, start cooking today with this amazing and easy cookbook.